LaVarenne®

TOUR BOOK

By Faye Levy

Peanut Butter Publishing

PEANUT BUTTER PUBLISHING
Peanut Butter Towers   Seattle, Washington 98134

TOUR BOOK

By Faye Levy

Editor: Judith Hill
Assistant Editor: Janet Jones
Drawings: Sarah Kensington
Cover Photography: Michael Montgomery

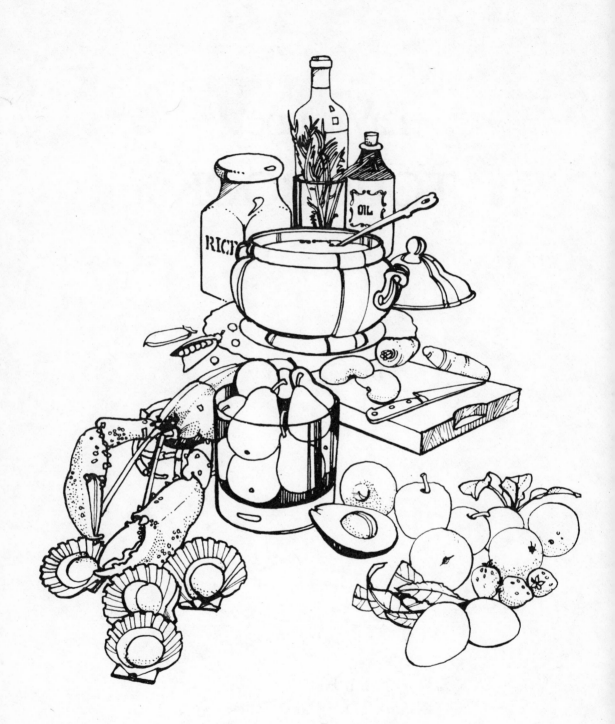

Contents

Ingredient quantities are given in U.S. standard measures with the rounded metric equivalents in parentheses.

ALL RECIPES SERVE FOUR UNLESS OTHERWISE STATED.

Introduction

A professional cook can be relied upon to give an acceptable, even excellent, rendering of any recipe in the standard repertoire. But memorable cooking has something more: a harmony, a balance and often a touch of fantasy that lifts it from the pedestrian to the brilliant. Into its making the chef has put his heart as well as his skill. He has made the dish his own.

This book is a collection of just such recipes chosen by the five of us who cook at La Varenne in Paris. These are the dishes we love to demonstrate on tour and to make at home. In their selections Chefs Fernand Chambrette and Claude Vauguet have kept mainly to cuisine—the first and main course dishes that form their *métier.* Chef Chambrette is famous for his preparation of fish, but his choice runs the gamut of peasant soups like *cotriade,* through the classics and on to the surprises of nouvelle cuisine. Chef Claude's choice, in keeping with his age, is more youthful. With his classical training he blends new ideas to fit modern tastes. And Chef Jorant, of course, keeps to his great love—*pâtisserie,* sweet, savory, simple and grand.

The recipes chosen by Gregory Usher and myself are different: French cooks by adoption, our ambitions are on a smaller scale. We favor dishes with a simple appeal that use few ingredients, and often ones that can be prepared ahead. But the theme is still unmistakably French. Gregory loves hearty regional dishes—especially lamb, rabbit and beef *ragoûts*—while mine is perhaps a lighter, more fanciful choice.

Each of us has a chapter in this book that is a snapshot of us and our cooking. The photographer, as it were, is Faye Levy. This is the team which has made La Varenne.

Which chef's choice would be yours? Try each and see.

Anne Willan

ANNE WILLAN

ECOLE DE CUISINE LA VARENNE
34 rue St. Dominique, 75007 Paris, France

FERNAND
CHAMBRETTE

Getting to know Chef Fernand Chambrette, the director of La Varenne, is a study in contrasts. He professes a cynical attitude toward life, yet has to bite his lower lip to keep from laughing at his own jokes. When not taking the cynic's stance, Chef Chambrette will sometimes maintain that he is a man of great simplicity and little knowledge. At others, though, he'll recommend an obscure book on the history of the French peasantry or tell you just how to test a wine to determine whether or not it has been chaptalized.

Chambrette began training for his career as a chef at twelve, when he entered the Ecole Hôtelière. By fifteen he was ready for an apprenticeship and later became an assistant chef at Prunier, the well-known Parisian fish restaurant. After the war, in 1946, he bought the Boule d'Or and became famous for his own fine fish dishes. With Chambrette as owner and chef, the restaurant was awarded two Michelin stars.

Chef Chambrette retired from the restaurant business in 1975 and came to La Varenne the following year. He teaches the perfectly prepared dishes for which his restaurant was known—*consommé Germiny, vol au vent aux fruits de mer, suprême de bar à l'oseille, soufflé au citron*—and also continues to invent. He finds fruit, a chicken left in the refrigerator or a cabbage that must be used, reflects for a few moments, and *voilà*. . .a new dish. Once at the end of a recipe testing session, he came along, picked up the bits left from the vegetable and seafood quiches being prepared and came up with a quiche that was better than any of those being tested.

The chef is pleased with the recognition he has received for his creativity in the kitchen, but when it is suggested that he is an artist, he mocks, "That makes me laugh. When I started, cooking was a job. Now the chefs are movie stars. It's getting so fashionable we're going to have to develop our own Beverly Hills."

Which side of Chambrette will be on show at a given moment is anyone's guess. Studying under him is doubly fascinating, for his knowledge of cooking and his attitudes toward life are equally diverse.

FERNAND CHAMBRETTE

Appetizers
Salad of Artichoke Bottoms and Mushrooms
Eggs in Red Wine Sauce

Main Courses
Breton Fish Soup
Trout à l'Italienne
Stuffed Sole with Whiskey Sauce
Salmon Escalopes with Spinach Mousse
Salmon Coulibiac
Lobster à l'Alsacienne
Chicken en Cocotte Vallée d'Auge
Chicken Suprêmes La Varenne
Duck Ragoût with Pears
Sautéed Sweetbreads with Glazed Root Vegetables
Tournedos with Stuffed Mushrooms Ali Bab
Veal Shoulder with Baby Vegetables

Vegetables
Carrot Purée with Mint
Turnip Purée
Broccoli Purée
Cauliflower Purée

Desserts
Lemon Mousse with Caramel Sauce
Macaroons
Praline Soufflé Crêpes
Rum Babas

Salad of Artichoke Bottoms and Mushrooms
FONDS D'ARTICHAUTS AUX CHAMPIGNONS

The French refer to the preparation of artichoke bottoms as "turning artichokes." Chef Chambrette illustrates this technique as, with perfect coordination, he deftly turns the artichoke with one hand and cuts off the leaves with the other. The mushroom salad may also be served on its own.

Salt
1 lemon
4 large artichokes
¼ pound (125 g) mushrooms, very thinly sliced
1 tablespoon chopped chives or parsley (for sprinkling)

For the Dressing:
1 teaspoon lemon juice
1 tablespoon wine vinegar
Salt and freshly ground pepper
4 tablespoons heavy cream
1 clove garlic, finely chopped

Bring a large pan of salted water to a boil. *To prepare the artichoke bottoms:* Add the juice of half a lemon to a bowl of cold water. Break the stem of each artichoke. Using a very sharp knife and holding it against the side of the artichoke, cut off all the large bottom leaves, leaving a soft cone of small leaves in the center. Trim this level with the end of the artichoke base. Rub sides of the base well with a cut lemon to prevent discoloration. Trim the base to an even round, slightly flattened on the bottom. Rub with cut lemon and drop into the bowl of cold lemon water.

To cook the artichoke bottoms: Drain the artichokes and add to the boiling water with the juice from the lemon half used to rub them. Simmer 15–20 minutes or until tender. Leave them to cool to tepid in the liquid; then drain and scoop out the central choke with a teaspoon.

For the dressing: Whisk the lemon juice and vinegar with salt and pepper and gradually whisk in the cream. Add the garlic. Pour over the sliced mushrooms, mix well, cover tightly and marinate at room temperature at least 2 hours. Both artichokes and mushrooms can be prepared up to 24 hours ahead. Keep tightly covered in the refrigerator.

Not more than 1–2 hours before serving: Arrange the artichoke bottoms on individual plates, taste the mushrooms for seasoning and pile them in the middle of the artichokes. Sprinkle with chopped chives or parsley just before serving.

Eggs in Red Wine Sauce
OEUFS POCHES EN MEURETTE

If violet-colored eggs bother you, use the wine in the sauce but poach the eggs in water acidulated with a spoonful of vinegar. To check whether or not an egg is correctly poached, lift it on a slotted spoon and touch the yolk gently—if it is still soft but slightly firmer than when raw, it is done.

8 very fresh eggs
2 tablespoons chopped parsley (for sprinkling)

For the Sauce:
3 cups (7.5 dl) red wine
1 cup (2.5 dl) veal stock
Bouquet garni
1 clove garlic, peeled
2 shallots, thinly sliced
3 tablespoons (45 g) butter
4 tablespoons (30 g) flour
Salt and freshly ground black pepper
Pinch of sugar— optional

For the Garnish:
⅓ pound (150 g) piece lean bacon, Canadian bacon or ham,
   cut in dice (lardons)
3 tablespoons (45 g) butter
16–20 baby onions—optional
¼ pound (125 g) mushrooms, quartered
Salt and freshly ground black pepper
8 slices French bread (½" or 1 cm thick) or white bread,
   cut in rounds
3 tablespoons oil and 3 tablespoons (45 g) butter, mixed
   (for frying)
1 clove garlic, peeled—optional

The recipe serves 8 as an appetizer or 4 as a light main dish.

For the sauce: In a sauté pan or shallow casserole, bring the wine, stock, bouquet garni, garlic and shallots to a boil. Poach the eggs in two batches in this mixture for 3–4 minutes. Drain on paper towels and trim. Boil the wine mixture until reduced by half.

For the garnish: Fry the bacon or ham in 1 tablespoon butter until lightly browned and drain on paper towels. Add the baby onions and sauté, shaking the pan often, until brown. Remove from the pan. Fry the mushrooms in the remaining butter until tender and sprinkle with salt and pepper. Make the croûtes by frying the bread in oil and butter until golden brown on both sides. Drain on paper towels and rub with a cut garlic clove.

To finish the sauce: With a fork mash the butter with the flour until smooth. Strain the wine mixture into a saucepan, bring to a boil and whisk in enough of the butter-flour mixture, piece by piece, so the sauce thickens to a light coating consistency. Simmer 2–3 minutes, add the mushrooms, onions and bacon, bring back to a boil and simmer 5–6 more minutes. Taste for seasoning—this sauce should be highly seasoned. If it is too acidic, add a tiny pinch of sugar. The eggs can be kept up to 30 minutes, and the sauce can be reheated.

Heat the oven to 350°F (175°C). Just before serving, arrange the croûtes on a platter, top with the eggs and put in the hot oven 1–2 minutes to reheat them. Coat with the very hot sauce and sprinkle with parsley.

Breton Fish Soup

COTRIADE BRETONNE

This dish is actually half-way between a soup and a stew. The generous amount of cream is typical of Chef Chambrette's recipes. Blanched watercress or spinach can be substituted for the sorrel and added with the mussels.

> 3 pounds (1.5 kg) mixed fish—monkfish, whiting, sole, turbot, mackerel, conger eel
> 1 quart (1 L) fish stock (see **Stuffed Sole with Whiskey Sauce**)
> 4 potatoes
> 2 onions, chopped
> 2 leeks, chopped
> 2 cloves garlic, chopped
> 2–4 tablespoons (30–60 g) butter
> Salt and pepper
> Bouquet garni
> 1 pound (500 g) raw or 1 cup (2.5 dl) cooked sorrel
> 3 cups (7.5 dl) mussels, cleaned
> 1 cup (2.5 dl) heavy cream
>
> **For the Croûtes:**
> 6–8 slices white bread, cut in heart shapes, crusts discarded
> 6 tablespoons (1 dl) oil (for frying)
> 1 clove garlic

Fillet the fish and use the heads, tails and bones of all except the mackerel to make the fish stock. Cut the fish fillets into medium-sized cubes.

For the croûtes: Fry the bread in the oil until golden brown on both sides. Rub each croûte with garlic.

Quarter the potatoes and cut in thin slices. Chop the onions, leeks and garlic together and cook slowly in 2 tablespoons (30 g) of butter. Add the fish stock, salt, pepper, bouquet garni and potatoes and simmer about 5 minutes, or until the potatoes are partly cooked. Add the firm-fleshed fish, simmer 3–4 minutes and add the softer fish. Simmer all together about 5 more minutes.

If using raw sorrel, remove the stems, wash the leaves and cook them in 2 tablespoons (30 g) more butter about 15 minutes, stirring often, until very dry. When the fish are nearly tender, add the cooked sorrel, the mussels in their shells and the cream. Continue cooking just until the mussels open. Remove the bouquet garni and taste for seasoning. Serve the cotriade in a shallow bowl and the croûtes separately.

Trout à L'Italienne
TRUITE A L'ITALIENNE

A l'Italienne does not mean that this recipe is Italian, but that it makes use of typically Italian ingredients.

3 shallots, finely chopped
Salt and freshly ground black pepper
4 large trout
2 very thin slices (2½ ounces or 75 g) prosciutto ham
2 very thin slices (2½ ounces or 75 g) cooked ham
3 tablespoons (45 g) butter
½ pound (250 g) mushrooms, very finely chopped
2 tomatoes, peeled, seeded and chopped
1 tablespoon tomato paste
3–4 leaves chopped fresh basil or pinch of dry basil
3–4 tablespoons veal stock or tomato sauce
¼ cup (30 g) dry breadcrumbs
Juice of ½ lemon

Fillets of salmon, sea bream, red mullet, whiting or turbot or steaks of tuna can also be used for this dish.

Butter an ovenproof platter generously. Sprinkle with two of the shallots, salt and pepper. Fillet the trout, remove the skin and put the fillets on the platter. Grind both types of ham together in a food processor or chop until the texture is as fine as possible.

Melt 1 tablespoon (15 g) of the butter, add the remaining shallot and cook slowly until soft but not browned. Add the mushrooms, a little salt and pepper and cook over high heat, stirring, until nearly all the liquid has evaporated. In another pan cook the tomatoes over high heat, stirring, about 10 minutes or again until nearly all the liquid has evaporated. Remove from the heat and add the mushrooms, tomato paste, ground ham, basil and veal stock or tomato sauce. Taste for seasoning and leave to cool. Spread the mixture over the fillets, completely covering them. Sprinkle with the breadcrumbs. Melt the remaining butter and sprinkle on top. The fish can be prepared ahead and kept one day in the refrigerator. It can also be frozen.

Twenty to thirty minutes before serving, set the oven at 450°F (230°C). Bake the trout 7–10 minutes or until tender when pierced with a fork. Squeeze lemon juice over the trout and serve. If the topping is not brown, brown lightly under the broiler.

Stuffed Sole with Whiskey Sauce
SOLE SOUFFLEE, SAUCE WHISKEY

Chef Chambrette reserves this intricate dish, which was popular in his restaurant, for advanced students. Special care must be taken in preparing the sole, so the white skin won't be pierced, and in making the sauce, so the yolks won't curdle and the butter won't melt.

4 small sole (¾–1 pound or 350–500 g each)
2 tablespoons whiskey

For the Fish Stock:
Heads and bones of the fish
1 medium onion, sliced
1 tablespoon (15 g) butter
1 quart (1 L) water
10 peppercorns
Bouquet garni

For the Filling:
7 ounces (200 g) pike or whiting fillets
1 egg white
2 tablespoons heavy cream
1½ teaspoons (7 g) salt
Pinch of pepper
Pinch of grated nutmeg

For the Sauce:
3 egg yolks
1½ tablespoons heavy cream
½ cup (125 g) cold butter, cut in cubes
¼ cup (6 cl) whiskey
3 tablespoons fish stock, or to taste
Salt
Pinch of cayenne

Cut the fins from the fish and trim the tails. Skin the dark side of the fish and scale the white side. Cut off the head and clean the fish. On the dark side, slit the length of the backbone; then detach the fillets from the center bone, leaving them attached at the outside edges. When the center bone is exposed, snip it with scissors at the head and tail. Snip the ends of each of the little bones attached to the center bone, thus freeing them somewhat from the flesh. Lastly, run a knife under these bones, gently freeing them from the flesh underneath. Without damaging the flesh, carefully pull out the center bone with the little bones attached. Reserve the heads and bones for stock.

For the fish stock: In a saucepan cook the onion slowly in the butter until soft but not brown. Add the fish heads and bones, water, peppercorns and bouquet garni. Bring to a boil, skimming occasionally, and simmer uncovered 20 minutes. Strain.

For the filling: Grind the pike or whiting fillets using the fine plate and place in a metal bowl over ice to chill. Keeping the bowl over ice, add the egg white and mix well with a wooden spoon. Add the cream 1 tablespoon at a time and mix vigorously. Season with salt, pepper and nutmeg. Chill well. Test the mixture by poaching 1 teaspoon of it in water; if the mixture does not hold together, add another egg white.

Spread some of the filling in each fish, in the cavity left by the center bone. Fold the two fillets over the filling. NOTE: a little of the filling will show. Set the sole on a generously buttered baking dish and add enough fish stock to come half-way up the fish. Add the whiskey and cover the fish with buttered paper. The fish can be prepared 2–3 hours ahead and kept covered in the refrigerator.

About one hour before serving: Preheat the oven to 400°F (200°C). Bake the sole 15–20 minutes or until the fish flakes easily with a fork. Carefully remove each fish from the liquid and use a metal scraper or knife to cut off the little bones from the sides. Check each to be sure none of the center bone has been left at the head end.

For the sauce: In a heavy-based saucepan whisk the egg yolks, cream, butter and whiskey over low heat until the sauce is thick enough to coat a spoon. NOTE: this sauce curdles very easily. Gradually add fish stock to taste and season with salt and cayenne.

Arrange the fish on a round platter, with the tails facing inward. Coat with sauce and serve the rest separately.

Salmon Escalopes with Spinach Mousse
ESCALOPES DE SAUMON A LA MOUSSE D'EPINARDS

Chef Chambrette is a purist when it comes to salmon; he says he'd rather eat canned sardines than frozen salmon!

4-pound (2 kg) piece salmon, with bones
Fish stock (see **Stuffed Sole with Whiskey Sauce**)
4 shallots, finely chopped
½ cup (1.25 dl) dry white wine or vermouth
Salt and pepper
1 tablespoon heavy cream
1 cup (250 g) butter, cold
Few drops of lemon juice

For the Spinach Mousse:
2 pounds (1 kg) spinach
Salt and pepper
1 tablespoon (15 g) butter
Pinch of grated nutmeg
2 egg whites (to finish)

For this dish, the salmon can be replaced by turbot or other firm-fleshed fish. The recipe serves 6–8 as an appetizer or 4 as a main dish.

For the spinach mousse: Remove the stems and wash the spinach leaves. Blanch in a large pan of boiling salted water 2–3 minutes or until just tender. Refresh under cold running water, squeeze out the excess moisture and purée in an electric food processor. Return to a small saucepan with the butter. Heat, stirring constantly, 2–3 minutes or until all the water evaporates. Season with salt, pepper and nutmeg.

Fillet the salmon and remove the skin. Cut each fillet in thin diagonal slices (escalopes). Make the fish stock and strain. Set the oven at 350°F (175°C). Butter a sauté pan or shallow baking dish generously and sprinkle with the shallots. Place the salmon escalopes on top, pour over the white wine and enough fish stock to just cover and sprinkle with salt and pepper. Bring to a boil on top of the stove. Cover with buttered paper and poach in the oven for 2–3 minutes or until the fish is lightly cooked. Let cool slightly, then lift out the fish and dry on paper towels. Keep warm until ready to serve.

Boil the salmon cooking liquid with the remaining fish stock until reduced to 2–3 tablespoons. Add the cream and reduce again. Beat in the butter gradually in small pieces. Work sometimes over very low heat and sometimes off the heat, so that the butter softens and thickens the sauce without melting. Add lemon juice, salt and pepper. Keep warm on a rack over warm, not boiling, water while reheating the fish.

To finish: Cover the salmon platter with foil and reheat in a 400°F (200°C) oven just until hot. *Meanwhile, finish the spinach mousse:* Whip the egg whites until stiff. Bring the spinach puree to a boil, take from the heat and add the beaten egg whites, whisking vigorously. Return to a boil, still whisking vigorously, and remove from the heat. Taste for seasoning. Spread the mousse on a platter, arrange the salmon on top, spoon the sauce over fish and serve.

Salmon Coulibiac
COULIBIAC DE SAUMON

Although of Russian origin, this dish has been "naturalized" by French chefs. Chef Chambrette often surrounds the filling with crêpes before wrapping it in pastry. He sometimes uses brioche (see Brioches) for the pastry. If the salmon is very fresh, he does not pre-cook it.

For the Sour Cream Pastry Dough:
3¾ cups (500 g) flour
2 teaspoons (10 g) salt
¾ cup (200 g) unsalted butter
2 eggs
5–6 tablespoons sour cream
1 egg, beaten to mix with ½ teaspoon salt (for glaze)

For the Filling:
Fish stock (see **Stuffed Sole with Whiskey Sauce**)
1 pound (500 g) piece of salmon
Salt and pepper
2 tablespoons (30 g) butter
1 onion, finely chopped
1 cup (200 g) rice
2 tablespoons chopped parsley
6 hard-cooked eggs, sliced

For the Duxelles:
1 onion, finely chopped
3 tablespoons (45 g) butter
¾ pound (350 g) mushrooms, finely chopped
1 tablespoon chopped parsley
1 teaspoon chopped chives
Salt and pepper

For Serving:
1 cup (2.5 dl) sour cream
½ cup (125 g) melted butter

Fluted pastry wheel—optional

The recipe serves 8.

To make the sour cream pastry dough: Sift the flour onto a marble slab or board, make a large well in the center and add the salt, softened butter, eggs and 5 tablespoons sour cream. Mix the center ingredients until smooth.

Gradually draw in the flour to make a smooth dough; if it is dry, add up to 1 tablespoon more sour cream. Work the dough in small pieces with the heel of the hand until pliable, then press together to form a ball. Cover and chill 1–2 hours.

For the filling: Heat the oven to 350°F (175°C). Pour fish stock over the salmon in a baking dish, season with salt and pepper, cover with foil and bake 5 minutes. Cool, strain the liquid, add enough water to make 2 cups (5 dl) and reserve. Lift the salmon from the bone in pieces as large as possible, discarding the skin and bone. In a casserole heat 2 tablespoons (30 g) butter, cook the onion slowly until soft but not brown and stir in the rice. Cook, stirring, 1–2 minutes until the grains look transparent, then add the reserved salmon liquid. Bring to a boil, cover and bake in the heated oven 20 minutes. Take out and set aside, covered, for 10 minutes. Then stir lightly with a fork, taste for seasoning, add the chopped parsley and cool.

For the duxelles: In a sauté pan or skillet cook the onion in the butter until soft but not brown. Add the chopped mushrooms, stir and cook over high heat until all the moisture has evaporated. Take from the heat and stir in the parsley and chives with plenty of seasoning.

To assemble: Roll out the dough to a 16"x10" (40x25 cm) rectangle. Arrange half the rice in a 12"x3½" (30x9 cm) strip in the middle of the dough. Add the sliced eggs. Spread the duxelles mixture on top, then set the pieces of salmon neatly on top of that. Pile the remaining rice mixture on the salmon, molding it to make as tall and neat a rectangle as possible. Cut a 2" (5 cm) square from each corner of dough and brush the edges with egg glaze. Lift one long edge of the dough on top of the filling and fold over the opposite edge to enclose it. Press gently to seal the dough and fold over the ends to make a neat package. Roll the package over onto a baking sheet so that the joined ends are underneath.

Roll out the excess dough to a long strip and cut into narrow bands, preferably with a fluted wheel. Lay the bands over the coulibiac to decorate it and press a long band around the base to neaten it. The coulibiac can be prepared 24 hours ahead and kept, covered with plastic wrap in the refrigerator, or it can be frozen.

To finish: Chill the coulibiac 15 minutes. Set the oven at 400°F (200°C). Brush the coulibiac with glaze, poke 2 steam holes in the top and bake in the hot oven 15 minutes or until the pastry is lightly browned. Turn down the heat to 350°F(175°C) and continue baking 25–35 minutes or until a skewer inserted for 30 seconds in the center is hot to the touch when withdrawn. If the pastry browns too much, cover it loosely with foil. Transfer the coulibiac to a long platter or tray and cut into slices to show the layers of filling. Serve sour cream and melted butter separately.

Lobster à L'Alsacienne
HOMARD A L'ALSACIENNE

When this incredibly rich dish, Chef Chambrette's latest creation, was tested for the first time, it was a true feat of teamwork. The chef cut up and cooked the lobster while one trainee rolled the fresh noodles, another pounded the lobster butter and a third stirred the sauce. Last, all the trainees silently watched as the chef finished the dish. If working alone, you can prepare the various parts step by step, then assemble the dish before serving.

2 live lobsters (2 pounds or 1 kg each)
1¼ cups (300 g) butter
1 onion, finely chopped
1 carrot, finely chopped
3 tablespoons oil
2 cups (5 dl) Gewürtztraminer wine
2 cups (5 dl) fish stock (see **Stuffed Sole with Whiskey Sauce**)
3 cups (7.5 dl) heavy cream
Salt and pepper
Few drops of lemon juice
Pinch of sugar
Pinch of cayenne pepper

For the Fresh Noodles:
1¾–2 cups (225–250 g) flour
2 large eggs

For the fresh noodles: Sift 1¾ cups (225 g) flour onto a working surface. Make a well in the center and add the eggs. Work in the flour with the fingertips, using a circular motion. When most of the flour has been incorporated by mixing, knead vigorously to gradually work in more flour to give a very stiff and dry dough. Continue kneading about 5 minutes or until the dough is elastic and nearly smooth. Put in a bowl, cover and chill about 30 minutes. Divide the dough into 3 or 4 pieces and work them through the widest setting on a pasta machine 5 or 6 times, folding it in three after each rolling, until very smooth. Next work it once through each of the thinner settings. Let dry 5 minutes and cut into noodles. Alternatively, divide the dough in half and roll out on a floured board to a very thin sheet. Let dry 30 minutes; then roll loosely and cut crosswise into ½" (1.25 cm) slices. Spread the noodles on a cloth or on paper, flour them lightly and leave to dry about 1 hour.

To kill live lobsters with a knife: Put each one in turn flat on a board, hard shell up, head to your right; cover the tail with a cloth. Hold the lobster firmly behind the head with your left hand and, with the point of a sharp, heavy knife, pierce down to the board through the cross mark that lies on the center of the head. The lobster is killed at once. Continue splitting the lobster body lengthwise as far as the tail; then cut the tail in 4 slices. Crack the claws. Save the liquid from the lobster. Discard the head sacs; scoop out the soft greenish meat and any black coral from the bodies of the lobsters and reserve in a small bowl.

In a large casserole melt 2 tablespoons (30 g) butter, add the onion and carrot and cook slowly until soft but not brown. In a large skillet, heat the oil, add the lobster pieces and sauté over high heat 2–3 minutes or until the shells turn red. Add the lobster pieces to the casserole with the wine, fish stock, 2 cups (5 dl) of the cream, lobster liquid, salt and pepper. Cover and boil 10 minutes. Remove the lobster pieces. Remove the meat from the tails and claws and cut it in large cubes. Crush the shells with a pestle or rolling pin, add one-third of them to the sauce and simmer 5 minutes.

With the remaining shells make lobster butter: Set the oven at 400°F (200°C). In a heavy-based pan put the remaining crushed shells and ⅓ cup (100 g) of the butter. Cook, stirring often, on the floor of the oven 15 minutes. Add enough cold water to nearly fill the pan and let rest 10–15 minutes. The lobster butter will come to the top. Skim it off and boil it in a small saucepan 5–10 minutes or until clear.

To cook the noodles: Bring a large pan of salted water to a boil. Add the noodles, bring back to a boil and simmer 1–2 minutes or until just tender (al dente). Drain the noodles and put in a saucepan with 2 tablespoons (30 g) butter, salt and pepper.

To finish: Reheat the sauce and add ⅓ cup (1 dl) cream. Whisk the remaining cream into the reserved internal meat and coral, then add this mixture to the sauce and cook over low heat, whisking, until it turns a bright pink. Strain through a fine strainer. Off the heat gradually whisk in the lobster butter. Add ½ cup (125 g) soft butter and stir it in so it softens but does not melt. Add a little lemon juice, and a pinch each sugar and cayenne. Taste for seasoning. In a separate saucepan, reheat the lobster pieces in the remaining butter. Add them to the hot sauce. Reheat the noodles and spoon onto a large platter. Spoon the lobster and sauce onto the bed of noodles and serve.

Chicken en Cocotte Vallée D'Auge

POULET EN COCOTTE VALLEE D'AUGE

The Auge Valley is in Normandy, famous for its cream, apples and Calvados.

2 tablespoons (30 g) butter
3½–4 pound (1.5–1.8 kg) whole roasting chicken, trussed
18–20 baby onions, peeled
Salt and pepper
½ pound (250 g) mushrooms, quartered
¼ cup (6 cl) Calvados
1 tablespoon chopped parsley (to finish)

For the Liaison:
3 egg yolks
1 cup (2.5 dl) heavy cream

Set the oven at 375°F (190°C). In a deep casserole melt the butter and brown the chicken on all sides. Take it out and brown the onions. Take them out, replace the chicken and sprinkle with salt and pepper. Cover and cook in the heated oven ¾–1 hour or until the juices run clear rather than pink when the thigh is pierced with a skewer. Add the onions 20 minutes before the end of cooking and the mushrooms 10 minutes before the end. The chicken can be prepared 2 days ahead, but it should be cooked only until barely done to allow for reheating. Keep it with the. vegetables in the casserole in the refrigerator.

To finish: Reheat the chicken and vegetables in a 350°F (175°C) oven if necessary. Pour over the Calvados, bring to a boil and flame. When the flame dies, transfer the chicken to a carving board and keep warm; leave the vegetables in the pan. Boil the cooking juices to a glaze and let cool slightly. *For the liaison:* Mix the yolks and cream and stir them into the cooled juices. Heat the sauce gently, stirring constantly, until it thickens. NOTE: if it gets too hot, it will curdle. Taste for seasoning and keep warm.

Carve the chicken and arrange it on a platter. Add reserved vegetables to the sauce and spoon them over the chicken. Sprinkle with chopped parsley and serve any remaining sauce separately.

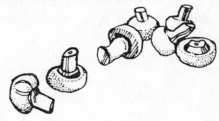

Chicken Suprêmes La Varenne
SUPREMES DE VOLAILLE LA VARENNE

François Pierre de la Varenne, the 17th century chef who has been called the founder of French classical cooking, created duxelles, a shallot-flavored mushroom purée.

4 chicken suprêmes
1 tablespoon heavy cream
1 cup (250 g) butter
Few drops lemon juice
Salt and pepper
Pinch of grated nutmeg

For the Duxelles:
4 ounces (120 g) fresh morels or 2 ounces (60 g) dried morels
8 ounces (250 g) mushrooms
Few drops lemon juice
Salt and pepper
1 tablespoon (15 g) butter
1 shallot, finely chopped
2 tablespoons heavy cream

For the duxelles: Soak dried morels 3–4 hours in cold water to cover, and drain. Wash fresh morels in several changes of water, brushing to remove all the sand. Put the mushrooms and morels in a pan with a few drops lemon juice, salt, pepper and water to cover. Cover and cook over high heat until the liquid boils to the top of the pan. Drain, reserving the liquid. Chop the morels and mushrooms until very fine or purée in a blender or electric food processor. Melt 1 tablespoon (15 g) butter, add the shallot and cook slowly until soft but not brown. Add the mushrooms, salt and pepper and cook over high heat, stirring, until nearly all the liquid has evaporated. Add cream, bring to a boil and reduce until thick but not dry.

For the sauce: Boil the mushroom cooking liquid until reduced to 2–3 tablespoons. Add 1 tablespoon cream and reduce again. Gradually beat in ⅔ cup (200 g) of the butter in small pieces. Work sometimes over very low heat and sometimes off heat, so the butter softens and thickens the sauce without melting. Add a few drops lemon juice, salt, pepper and nutmeg to taste. Keep warm on a rack over warm, not boiling, water while cooking the suprêmes.

Season the suprêmes with salt and pepper. Heat the remaining butter and cook the suprêmes over low heat 5–6 minutes on each side until tender but not brown. *To serve:* Spoon the mushroom purée onto a platter. Arrange the suprêmes on top and coat with the sauce.

Duck Ragoût with Pears

RAGOUT DE CANARD AUX POIRES

This recipe is another creation by Chef Chambrette—the result of a left-over duck and some extra pears. For an even better flavor, he suggests making brown stock for the sauce with the duck backs and wings.

> 1 large duck (4 pounds or 1.8 kg)
> 1 tablespoon oil
> 1 tablespoon (15 g) butter
> Salt and freshly ground black pepper
> 3 large pears
> 1 lemon
> 2 tablespoons brown sugar
> ¼ cup (6 cl) white wine vinegar
> ¾ cup (2 dl) basic brown sauce (see **Chicken Suprêmes with Port**)

Remove the wings of the duck. Remove the legs and cut each into two pieces at the joint. Cutting along the breastbone, remove the entire breast in one or two boneless pieces and trim off excess fat.

In a large sauté pan heat the oil and butter. Season the pieces of duck. Add the leg and thigh pieces to the hot fat and brown on all sides over high heat. Add the breast and brown it also. Continue cooking over low heat, turning occasionally, 20–30 minutes or until deep brown.

Peel and quarter the pears and rub with a cut lemon. Add them to the pan, cover and stew gently with the duck over low heat about 15 minutes. Transfer the pears to a platter—they should still be rather firm. Add the brown sugar, stir well over low heat and add the vinegar. Bring to a boil and simmer 10 minutes. Skim excess fat from the liquid and add the brown sauce. Simmer 15 minutes more and taste for seasoning. Return the pears to the sauce and simmer about 5 more minutes or until the duck and pears are tender. The duck can be cooked 48 hours ahead; keep it in the sauce, covered, in the refrigerator.

To serve: Reheat the duck if necessary. Slice the breast into thin strips and arrange on a platter. Arrange the leg and thigh pieces around them and garnish with the pears. Reheat the sauce, skim off excess fat and spoon the sauce over the duck.

Sautéed Sweetbreads with Glazed Root Vegetables
ESCALOPES DE RIS DE VEAU POELEES AUX RACINES

This dish was conceived by Chef Chambrette for La Varenne's graduate course. Besides its beauty and harmony of flavors, it is a test of a student's patience and ability to work quickly.

2–3 pairs (1½ pounds or 750 g) calves' sweetbreads
1 quart (1 L) water
1 carrot, sliced
1 onion, sliced
Bouquet garni
Salt and pepper
½ cup (75 g) flour
2 tablespoons oil
2 tablespoons (30 g) butter

For the Glazed Vegetables:
8 carrots
1 small celery root
4 turnips
6 tablespoons (90 g) butter
Salt and pepper
½ teaspoon sugar

For the Sauce:
¼ cup (6 cl) Madeira or sherry
1 cup (2.5 dl) basic brown sauce (see **Chicken Suprêmes with Port**)
2 tablespoons (30 g) butter (to finish)

Soak the sweetbreads 2–3 hours in cold water, changing the water once or twice. Drain, rinse and put them in a pan with the water, carrot, onion, bouquet garni, salt and pepper. Bring slowly to a boil, skimming occasionally, and simmer 10 minutes. Drain, rinse the sweetbreads and peel them, removing the ducts. Press them between 2 plates with a 2 pound (1 kg) weight on top and leave to cool completely.

For the vegetables: Cut the carrots into 1½" (about 4 cm) lengths and use a sharp paring knife to trim each piece to an olive shape. Shape the celery root and turnips in similar-sized olive-shaped pieces. In a sauté pan or shallow saucepan bring the carrots to a boil with 2 tablespoons (30 g) butter, salt, pepper, sugar and water to just cover. Simmer 15–20 minutes or until nearly tender. Boil rapidly until nearly all the liquid has evaporated. In another pan bring the celery root to a boil with 2 tablespoons (30 g) butter, salt, pepper and water to cover. Simmer 15–20 minutes or until nearly tender. In a third pan bring the turnips to a boil with the remaining 2 tablespoons (30 g) butter, salt, pepper and water to cover. Simmer 5–6 minutes or until nearly tender.

Cut the sweetbreads in ½" (1 cm) thick diagonal slices. Season and coat lightly in flour. In a large sauté pan or skillet heat the oil and butter and sauté the sweetbreads, in two batches if necessary, over medium heat 8–10 minutes or until tender and golden brown on both sides. Remove the sweetbreads and keep warm. Add the Madeira or sherry and the basic brown sauce to the pan and bring to a boil, stirring.

To finish: Reheat each of the root vegetables, boiling down the liquid until it becomes a glaze. Transfer the sweetbreads and vegetables to a platter, remove the sauce from the heat and whisk in the 2 tablespoons (30 g) butter, in small pieces. Serve the sauce separately.

Tournedos with Stuffed Mushrooms Ali Bab
TOURNEDOS DE L'ALI BAB

Ali Bab was a well-known French gourmet of the 1920s. This recipe can be varied in many ways, as he suggests: the ham can be replaced by tongue, the mushrooms by cèpes, morels or truffles, the veal stock by beef stock, the port by Madeira or sherry, and the croûtes of bread by croûtes of brioche or rounds of puff pastry.

4 tournedos steaks cut 1½–2" (about 4–5 cm) thick
4 thick slices bread (for croûtes)
3 tablespoons oil and 3 tablespoons (45 g)
   butter (for frying)

For the Sauce:
5 tablespoons (75 g) butter
4 tablespoons (30 g) flour
3 cups (7.5 dl) veal stock
Bouquet garni
1 teaspoon meat glaze—optional
Salt and freshly ground black pepper
⅓ cup (1 dl) port wine

For the Stuffed Mushrooms:
8–12 large mushrooms
1 cup (about 6 ounces or 180 g) cooked chopped ham or
    Canadian bacon
2 egg yolks
Juice of ½ lemon
Salt—optional
Pinch of pepper

For the sauce: In a saucepan melt 3 tablespoons (45 g) butter, add the flour and cook, stirring, until browned. Add the stock, bouquet garni, meat glaze and seasoning and bring to a boil, stirring. Simmer uncovered 30–45 minutes until the sauce is well-flavored and glossy. Add the port, strain and taste for seasoning.

For stuffed mushrooms: set the oven at 350°F (175°C). Remove the mushroom stems and chop them. Mix with the chopped ham or bacon, egg yolks, lemon juice and pepper to taste. (If the ham is well-flavored, no salt is needed.) Mound the mixture in the mushroom caps. Arrange the mushrooms in a baking dish and bake 15–20 minutes or until tender. Both sauce and mushrooms can be prepared up to 24 hours ahead and kept covered in the refrigerator.

To finish: If possible, have the steaks at room temperature. Cut rounds from the bread for croûtes the same diameter as the steaks. Reheat the mushrooms and sauce if necessary. In a heavy-based frying pan heat the oil and butter and fry the croûtes, turning them to brown both sides. Drain on paper towels. Pour off all but 2 tablespoons fat and fry the tournedos, allowing 3–4 minutes on each side for rare steak. Season the steaks after turning them. To finish the sauce, take it from the heat and whisk in the remaining 2 tablespoons (30 g) butter, a small piece at a time. Keep it hot but do not allow it to boil or it will separate.

Set the tournedos on the croûtes on a platter, spoon over a little sauce and set a mushroom on each one. Arrange the remaining mushrooms around the edge of the platter and serve the rest of the sauce separately.

Veal Shoulder with Baby Vegetables
EPAULE DE VEAU AUX PETITS LEGUMES

According to Chef Chambrette, chefs have been turning vegetables to an olive shape since the time of Louis XV, who had a dislike for straight edges.

4–5 pound (2–2.5 kg) boned shoulder of veal, with the bones
Salt and freshly ground black pepper
1 tablespoon oil
4 tablespoons (60 g) butter
1 onion, diced
1 carrot, diced
2 stalks celery, diced
1 cup (2.5 dl) white wine
2–3 cups (5–7.5 dl) veal stock
2 teaspoons tomato purée
1 clove garlic, crushed
Bouquet garni
2 tablespoons (15 g) flour
2 tablespoons chopped parsley (to finish)

For the Stuffing:
1 onion, chopped
2 tablespoons (30 g) butter
1 cup (50 g) fresh white breadcrumbs
¼ cup (6 cl) white wine
1 pound (500 g) finely ground pork, fat and lean mixed
2 cloves garlic, crushed
1 tablespoon chopped parsley
2 teaspoons chopped mixed herbs—tarragon, chives, thyme
Salt and freshly ground black pepper
1 egg, beaten to mix

For the Garnish:
1½ pounds (750 g) baby carrots, or large carrots, quartered or
    trimmed to an oval shape
1½ pounds (750 g) baby onions, blanched and peeled
2 pounds (1 kg) small new potatoes, peeled

If you like, carrots and onions can be glazed and the potatoes sautéed separately to be sure each cooks evenly and is not crushed by the meat. The recipe serves 6–8.

Set the oven at 350°F (175°C). *For the stuffing:* Cook the onion in the butter until soft but not brown and let cool. Moisten the breadcrumbs with the wine. Mix the pork with the onion, breadcrumbs, garlic, parsley, herbs and plenty of salt and pepper; stir in the beaten egg. Sauté a small piece and taste for seasoning. Lay the meat, cut side up, on a board and sprinkle with salt and pepper. Spread with the stuffing, roll and tie in a neat cylinder.

In a large casserole, heat the oil and 2 tablespoons (30 g) butter and brown the meat and bones on all sides. Take them out, add the diced onion, carrot and celery and cook over low heat 5–7 minutes until slightly soft. Replace the veal and bones, add the wine, 1 cup (2.5 dl) of the stock, tomato purée, garlic, bouquet garni, salt and pepper, cover and bring to a boil. Braise in the heated oven 1½ hours or until almost tender. Remove the meat and strain the sauce. *Replace the meat and cook the garnish:* Add the carrots, pour over the sauce and add more stock if necessary to cover them. Cover and continue cooking 20 minutes. Add the onions, potatoes and more stock to cover and continue cooking 20–25 minutes or until vegetables and meat are tender. The dish can be cooked 2–3 days ahead and kept in the refrigerator, but the vegetables should be slightly under-done to allow for reheating.

To finish: If necessary reheat the meat in a 350°F (175°C) oven. Remove the meat and vegetables and keep warm. Skim any fat from the sauce, taste for seasoning and reduce if necessary until well-flavored. Cream the remaining butter with the flour and whisk it into the sauce, piece by piece, cooking until it thickens. Strain into a saucepan and keep hot. Discard the strings, cut the meat in ³/₈" (1 cm) slices and arrange them overlapping on a platter. Spoon the vegetables around and coat the meat and vegetables with a little sauce. Sprinkle the vegetables with chopped parsley and serve the remaining sauce separately.

Carrot Purée with Mint
PUREE CRECY A LA MENTHE

In spite of the hard work involved, Chef Chambrette forces all vegetable purées through a drum sieve to ensure a perfectly smooth texture.

> 1½ pounds (750 g) carrots
> Salt and pepper
> 1 tablespoon (15 g) butter
> ½–1 teaspoon sugar—optional
> ¼ cup (6 cl) heavy cream
> 1 tablespoon chopped mint leaves

Peel and slice the carrots. Bring to a boil in salted water to cover and cook 8–10 minutes or until very tender when pierced with skewer. Drain and purée them in a blender or electric food processor or work them through a food mill.

In a pan melt the butter, add the carrot purée and heat. Add sugar, salt and pepper and beat in the cream a little at a time. Add the mint and taste for seasoning. The purée can be made 2–3 days ahead and kept covered in the refrigerator.

To serve: Reheat the purée if necessary. Pile in a bowl and mark the top in waves with a knife.

Turnip Purée
PUREE FRENEUSE

Potatoes that have been chilled and reheated invariably taste stale, so do not make any purée containing them more than a couple of hours before serving.

> 4 tablespoons (60 g) butter
> 3–4 medium turnips (1 pound or 500 g), peeled and thinly sliced
> 2 medium potatoes (½ pound or 250 g)
> 1 cup (2.5 dl) milk
> Salt and pepper
> Pinch of grated nutmeg
> 1 tablespoon heavy cream—optional

In a heavy-based pan melt 3 tablespoons (45 g) butter, add the turnips and cover with foil and the lid. Cook gently, stirring occasionally, 10–15 minutes until slightly soft but not brown.

Peel the potatoes and cut in thin slices. Do not soak them in water as this removes some of their starch. Add them to the softened turnips with the milk, salt, pepper and nutmeg. Cover and simmer 15–20 minutes or until the vegetables are very tender. Drain them and purée in a blender or an electric food processor or work through a food mill. Discard the milk or use it for soup. The purée can be prepared up to 2 hours ahead. Keep it warm in a water bath or covered at room temperature.

To finish: Reheat the purée if necessary and taste for seasoning. Beat in the remaining 1 tablespoon (15 g) butter and the cream. Serve as soon as possible.

Broccoli Purée
PUREE DE BROCOLIS

Two or three vegetable purées of different colors make an attractive garnish for roasted, grilled or sautéed meats. Purées are especially appealing served in boat-shaped pastry shells (see **Morel Boats***).*

> 1 bunch (about 2 pounds or 1 kg) broccoli
> Salt and pepper
> 2 tablespoons (30 g) butter
> Pinch of grated nutmeg
> 1–2 tablespoons heavy cream

Divide the broccoli into pieces and peel the thick outer skin from the ends of the stems so they cook evenly. Cook in boiling salted water 7–10 minutes or until just tender. Drain very thoroughly and purée in a blender or electric food processor, or work through a food mill. The purée can be prepared a day ahead and kept covered in the refrigerator.

To finish: Melt the butter, add the purée with nutmeg, salt and pepper and cook, stirring, until very hot. Stir in the cream and taste for seasoning; the purée should be just soft enough to fall from the spoon.

Cauliflower Purée
PUREE DUBARRY

Substitute a medium cauliflower for the broccoli.

Lemon Mousse with Caramel Sauce

MOUSSE DE CITRON, SAUCE CARAMEL

Chef Chambrette insists that the lemon mixture be beaten until extremely thick and tells students tired from whisking, "It'll be thick enough when you can write your name with it."

For the Mousse:
1 envelope (¼ ounce or 7 g) gelatin
½ cup (1.25 dl) water
2 eggs
2 egg yolks
⅓ cup (75 g) sugar
Grated rind and juice of 2 lemons
1 cup (2.5 dl) heavy cream, whipped until it holds a soft shape

For the Caramel Sauce:
1 cup (200 g) sugar
½ cup (1.25 dl) cold water
½ cup (1.25 dl) warm water

For Decoration:
1 cup (2.5 dl) heavy cream
1 tablespoon sugar
1 teaspoon vanilla extract
5–6 candied violets—optional

Ring or kugelhopf mold (1 quart or 1 L capacity)
Pastry bag with medium star tube

For the mousse: Dampen the ring mold (preferably of tin-lined copper or stainless steel). Sprinkle the gelatin over the water in a small pan and let stand 5 minutes until spongy. Combine the eggs and yolks and gradually beat in the sugar, grated lemon rind and lemon juice. Set the bowl over a pan of simmering water and beat with a whisk or rotary beater 5–8 minutes or until the mixture is light and thick enough to leave a ribbon trail when the beater is lifted. Take from the heat and continue beating. Meanwhile, melt the gelatin over low heat, beat into the warm lemon mixture and continue beating until cool.

Set the bowl over a pan of ice water and chill it, stirring occasionally, until the mixture starts to set. Fold in the lightly whipped cream and pour into the mold. Cover and chill at least 2 hours or until firmly set. The mousse can be kept up to 24 hours in the refrigerator.

For the caramel sauce: Heat the sugar and cold water until dissolved, bring to a boil and cook steadily to a rich brown caramel. It must be well browned, but do not let it burn. Take from the heat and at once add the warm water, standing back because the caramel will sputter. Heat gently to melt the caramel and let cool. The caramel can be prepared 24 hours ahead.

Up to 2 hours before serving: Dip the mold in hot water for a few seconds, run a small knife around the edge of the mousse to release the air-lock and unmold onto a platter. *To decorate:* In a chilled bowl whip the cream until it starts to thicken. Add the sugar and vanilla and continue beating until the cream holds a shape and sticks to the whisk. Using a pastry bag fitted with a star tube, pipe rosettes of whipped cream onto the mousse and a ruffle around the base. Top rosettes with the candied violets. Keep in the refrigerator. Serve the caramel sauce separately.

Macaroons

MACARONS

Macaroons are Chef Chambrette's favorite cookie.

    1 cup (125 g) almonds, blanched and peeled
    1½–2 egg whites
    ¾ cup (160 g) sugar
    ½ teaspoon vanilla extract
    2 tablespoons confectioners' sugar, sifted (for sprinkling)

The recipe makes about 12 macaroons.

Line a heavy baking sheet with greased parchment paper. Set the oven at 400°F (200°C). Grate the almonds in a cheese grater. Using a mortar with pestle, pound the almonds, adding ½ an egg white a tablespoon at a time. Pound to a smooth and very fine paste. Add half the sugar and incorporate it into the mixture, using the pestle. Next add another ½ egg white and continue working with the pestle. In the same way incorporate the remaining sugar, then another ½ egg white. Beat in the vanilla. NOTE: the dough should be soft but not runny. If necessary add a little more egg white.

Using your hands, roll the mixture into balls the size of walnuts. Arrange on the prepared baking sheets and flatten slightly. Brush with a little water and sprinkle each with confectioners' sugar. Bake in the top third of the heated oven 18–20 minutes, or until the tops are lightly browned. Lift one end of the paper slightly, immediately pour a glass of water under the paper and stand back. NOTE: the hot baking sheet turns the water into steam, making it easy to remove the macaroons. After a few moments remove the macaroons from the paper and transfer to a rack to cool. They can be stored 1–2 weeks in an airtight container, but they tend to harden.

Praline Soufflé Crêpes
CREPES SOUFFLEES PRALINEES

When watching Chef Chambrette beating egg whites with all his energy, it may seem they are stiff enough; but he continues on and on, switching hands but never stopping, until they form perfectly stiff, glossy peaks.

For the Crêpes:
1 cup (125 g) flour
⅓ teaspoon (2 g) salt
1 cup (2.5 dl) milk
3 eggs
2 tablespoons (30 g) melted butter or oil
¼ cup (60 g) clarified butter or oil (for frying)

For the Praline:
½ cup (100 g) sugar
½ cup (100 g) whole unblanched almonds

For the Soufflé Mixture:
1 cup (2.5 dl) milk
½ cup (100 g) sugar
1 vanilla bean
3 egg yolks
5 tablespoons (40 g) flour
4 egg whites

The recipe makes 16–18 crêpes to serve 6–8.

For the crêpes: Sift the flour into a bowl, make a well in the center and add the salt and half the milk. Gradually whisk in the flour to make a smooth batter; then whisk in the eggs. NOTE: do not beat the batter too much or the finished crêpes will be tough. Stir in the melted butter or oil with half the remaining milk, cover and let the batter stand 1–2 hours.

Just before using, stir in enough of the remaining milk to make a batter the consistency of thin cream. Brush or rub a crêpe pan with butter or oil and heat until very hot. Add 2–3 tablespoons batter to the pan and turn it quickly so the bottom is evenly coated. Brown one side over fairly high heat, turn and brown the other side. Turn out onto a plate and continue with the remaining crêpes, greasing the pan occasionally. The crêpes can be made ahead and kept, layered with waxed paper, for up to 3 days in the refrigerator. They can also be frozen.

For the praline: In a heavy-based pan heat the sugar and almonds, stirring occasionally, until the sugar melts and starts to caramelize. Continue cooking over low heat, stirring, until deep brown and the almonds pop, showing they are toasted. NOTE: do not allow praline to burn. Immediately pour the mixture onto an oiled baking sheet and let it cool and harden. When crisp, work it to a powder a little at a time in a blender, food processor, or rotary cheese grater.

For the soufflé base: Heat the milk with half the sugar and the vanilla bean. Beat the rest of the sugar with the yolks until thick and stir in the flour. Beat the boiling milk into the yolk mixture. Return to the pan and cook, whisking constantly, until thick. Keep the mixture, with a piece of waxed paper pressed on top, in the refrigerator.

To finish: About ½ hour before serving, set the oven at 375°F (190°C). Beat the egg whites until very stiff. Meanwhile, heat the yolk mixture until hot to the touch. Fold it and the praline in to the whites as lightly as possible. Put about 2 tablespoons soufflé mixture on each crêpe, fold in half or roll loosely and set on a buttered heatproof platter. Bake immediately for 10–12 minutes until puffed. Serve at once.

Rum Babas
BABAS AU RHUM

Babas are said to have been invented by Stanislaus Leszczynski, the 17th century King of Lorraine, when he sprinkled his dry kugelhopf with rum. It was so good he called it after Ali Baba, the hero of his favorite romance.

1 package dry yeast, or 1 cake (15 g) compressed yeast
3 tablespoons lukewarm water
1¾ cups (225 g) flour
3 eggs, beaten to mix
1 teaspoon (5 g) salt
1 tablespoon (15 g) sugar
½ cup (125 g) unsalted butter, softened
⅔ cup (75 g) dried currants
½ cup (1.25 dl) rum
¼ cup (6 cl) water

For the Syrup:
2½ cups (500 g) sugar
1 quart (1 L) water

8 dariole molds

Dariole molds are bucket-shaped; any small deep molds can be substituted. The recipe serves 8.

Sprinkle or crumble the yeast over the lukewarm water and let stand 5 minutes or until dissolved. Sift the flour into a warm bowl, make a well in the center and add the yeast mixture, eggs, salt and sugar. Work to a smooth dough with the hand. Knead by lifting the dough with the fingers and throwing it back into the bowl for 5 minutes or until smooth and elastic. Put the soft butter in pieces on top of the dough. Cover the bowl with a damp cloth and leave to rise in a warm place ¾–1 hour or until doubled in bulk. Soak the dried currants in ¼ cup (6 cl) rum and the water.

Set the oven at 400°F (200°C). Butter the molds, chill them in the freezer and butter them again.

Beat the softened butter into the risen dough until smooth; then drain the currants and add. Drop the dough from a spoon into the molds to fill them by one-third. Set them on a baking sheet, cover with a cloth and let rise in a warm place 50–60 minutes or until the molds are almost full. Check to make sure the dough does not stick to the cloth. Bake in heated oven 20 minutes or until they begin to shrink from the sides of the molds. Unmold and let cool. The babas can be baked up to 2 weeks before serving and kept in an airtight container or they can be frozen. The drier they are, the more rum syrup they absorb.

For the syrup: Heat the sugar with the water over low heat until dissolved; then boil about 2–3 minutes or until the syrup is clear. Take from the heat and add the babas. Carefully turn them over several times to make sure they absorb as much syrup as possible. They will swell and be very shiny. Using a large slotted spoon, carefully transfer them to a rack. Reserve the remaining syrup for serving. Babas keep well, tightly covered, up to 24 hours.

Just before serving, sprinkle a little rum over the babas. Add the remaining rum to the reserved syrup and serve separately.

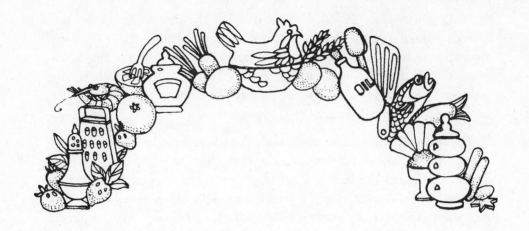

ALBERT
JORANT

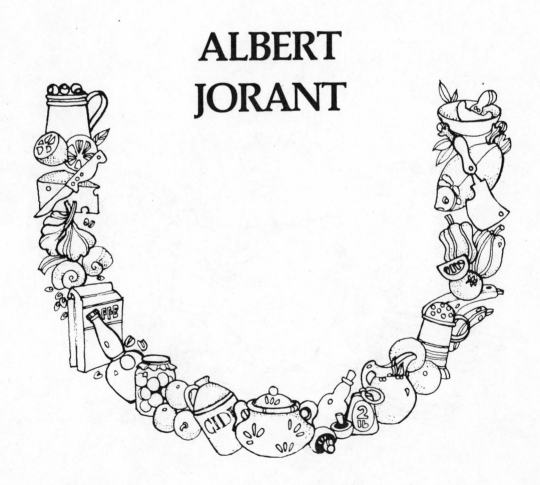

Albert Jorant enters a classroom quickly with a light step and winks all around. He's usually already rubbing his hands together in anticipation of the day's baking. Chef Jorant can make a pound of pâté brisée (pie pastry) in exactly two minutes twenty seconds. And as he works he never stops talking. He is La Varenne's chef *pâtissier*, and his talk is of pastry. Jorant often says smilingly that he speaks continually so no one in the audience will fall asleep, but there's little chance of that in his fast-moving demonstrations. After fifty years in the business, he explains, it's natural that he has a few tips to pass on.

His career began in 1930 when, at thirteen, he was apprenticed to a caterer. Jorant worked for the next four years without a single day off. At seventeen he accepted his first job as an assistant chef with a bakery and catering house. He was a navy cook during his military service and then returned to baking and catering as a chef and manager until 1952 when he opened his own catering house, which he ran for twenty years.

Then, turned demonstrator and instructor, the chef spent four years at the Cordon Bleu in Paris before joining La Varenne in 1976. He is a natural teacher who insists that, though there may be many good methods in *pâtisserie*, students should follow his because they're best. His students are believers because even the impressive displays of the *pâtisseries* of Paris pale before one of Jorant's ethereal cakes, perfect tarts, or his delicately decorated petits fours.

ALBERT JORANT

Appetizers
Cocktail Puff Pastries
Vegetable Julienne Pie
Mushroom Bouchées

Main Courses
Sea Bass in Pastry
Braised Ham with Spinach in Pastry
Lamb Chops in Puff Pastry

Molded Desserts
Coffee Bavarian Cream
Chocolate Charlotte

Petits Fours
Almond Petits Fours
Russian Cigarettes
Raisin Cookies
Florentines
Ladyfingers

Cakes
Strawberry Mousse Cake
Singapore Cake
Rolled Sponge Cake with Chocolate Filling
Almond Meringue Cake

Sweet Pastries
Cream Puffs with Chocolate Sauce
Gâteau Paris-Brest
Brioches
Swiss Brioche
Sweet Puff Pastries
Gâteau Pithiviers
Croissants

Cocktail Puff Pastries
FEUILLETES POUR COCKTAIL

Chef Jorant teaches that in French cooking there is actually a small number of basic preparations. Once you know them, you can put them together in any way you like and develop new variations. For example, instead of anchovies, these puff pastries can be spread with chopped sautéed livers or foie gras pâté before being folded and cut into fingers. For cheese fingers the pastry can be left in one layer and sprinkled with grated Parmesan or Gruyère cheese before being cut.

    1 egg, beaten to mix with ½ teaspoon salt (for glaze)
    Chosen filling (see below)

For the Puff Pastry Dough:
1 cup (250 g) unsalted butter
2 cups (250 g) flour
1 teaspoon (5 g) salt
1 teaspoon lemon juice—optional
½–⅔ cup (1.25–2 dl) ice water

For the puff pastry: If possible use unbleached pastry flour. Soften 2 tablespoons (30 g) butter, but keep the remaining butter cold. Sift the flour onto a cold marble slab or board, make a well in the center and add the salt, lemon juice, ½ cup (1.25 dl) water and softened butter. Work these ingredients until mixed; then gradually work in the flour, using fingertips to pull the dough into large crumbs. If the crumbs are dry, add a little more water; the amount depends on the type of flour used. Do not knead, but cut the dough several times with a dough scraper to ensure that the ingredients are evenly blended. Press into a ball; it should be quite soft. Wrap and chill 15 minutes.

Lightly flour the cold butter and pound it flat with a rolling pin. Fold it and continue pounding and folding until pliable but not sticky. Shape it into a 6" (15 cm) square and flour it lightly. Roll out the dough on a floured surface to a 12" (30 cm) square. Set the butter in the center and fold the dough around it like an envelope. Turn this "package" over so the seams are down and tap a few times with rolling pin to flatten it slightly.

Roll it to a rectangle 7–8" (17–20 cm) wide and 18–20" (45–50 cm) long. Keeping the edges as even as possible, fold in thirds with one end inside, as in folding a business letter. Seal the edges by pressing with rolling pin and turn the dough a quarter turn (90°) to bring the closed seam to your left side so the dough opens like a book. This is called a "turn." Roll out again and fold in 3 for the second turn. Wrap the dough and chill 15 minutes.

Give the dough 6 turns in all with a 15 minute rest in the refrigerator between every 2 turns. Chill at least 15 minutes before using. After 4 or 6 turns, the dough can be kept, tightly wrapped, up to 4 days in the refrigerator or up to 3 months in the freezer.

Roll out the dough slightly thinner than ¼" (6 mm) thick, fill with chosen filling and shape according to individual recipe. Set on a dampened baking sheet and chill 15 minutes. Set the oven at 425°F (220°C). Bake the pastries in the preheated oven 8–12 minutes or until puffed and brown; transfer to a rack to cool.

The pastries are best eaten the day they are baked, but they can be kept a day or two in an airtight container. They can also be frozen, baked or unbaked.

Anchovy Fingers
ALLUMETTES AUX ANCHOIS

Roll the dough to strips 6" (15 cm) wide and cut in half lengthwise, trimming the edges. Brush one rectangle with egg glaze and lay 30 drained anchovy fillets crosswise on it at 1½" (about 4 cm) intervals. Place the second rectangle on top and press down gently with a fingertip to outline anchovies. Brush with egg glaze and cut between each fillet to form fingers. Decorate each in a lattice pattern with the back of a knife, chill and bake as above. Makes about 30 fingers.

Ham Crescents
CROISSANTS AU JAMBON

Roll the dough to a strip 6" (15 cm) wide, trim the edges, cut in half lengthwise, then crosswise to form 3" (7.5 cm) squares. Chop ¾ cup (100 g) prosciutto or cooked ham and mix with a little Worcestershire sauce. Cut each square into two triangles and in the center put a teaspoon of the ham mixture. Roll up the triangles, starting at the long edge; then roll on the table with your hand to elongate the roll slightly and seal it. Shape into a crescent on a dampened baking sheet. Brush with egg glaze, chill and bake as above. Makes about 30 crescents.

Vegetable Julienne Pie
TARTE A LA JULIENNE DE LEGUMES

The chef admits that he seldom follows recipes for fillings (although he insists that the proportions for a dough be followed to the letter). In this recipe, he often uses other vegetables or replaces the julienne mixture with slices of cheese.

For the Dough:
3–3¼ cups (375–400 g) flour
1 package dry yeast, or 1 cake (15 g) compressed yeast
½ cup (1.25 dl) lukewarm milk
3 eggs
1½ teaspoons (7 g) salt
½ cup (125 g) butter, softened

For the Filling:
2 carrots
3 large leeks
½ pound (250 g) mushroom caps
5 ounces (150 g) ham, thinly sliced
3 tablespoons (45 g) butter
Salt and pepper

For the Custard:
3 eggs
1 cup (2.5 dl) heavy cream
Salt and pepper
Pinch of grated nutmeg

Two 8-9" (20-23 cm) pie pans or layer pans

The recipe serves 8–10.

Sift the flour into a bowl, make a well in the center and crumble in the yeast. Pour ¼ cup (6 cl) milk over yeast and let stand 5 minutes or until dissolved. Add the remaining milk, eggs and salt. Beat with the hand, gradually drawing in enough flour to make a dough that is soft and slightly sticky. Knead the dough by slapping it against the sides of the bowl or on a marble slab 5 minutes or until very elastic. Beat in the very soft butter. Transfer to an oiled bowl and cover with a damp cloth. Let rise in warm place 1–1½ hours or until doubled in bulk.

For the filling: Cut the carrots, the white part of the leeks, mushroom caps and ham in thin julienne strips 1½" (about 4 cm) long. In a sauté pan melt the butter, add the carrots and leeks with salt and pepper. Cover and

45

cook over low heat for 15 minutes, stirring often. Add the mushrooms and continue cooking, stirring often, about 10 minutes more or until all the vegetables are tender. Stir in the ham and taste for seasoning. *For the custard:* Beat the eggs with the cream, salt, pepper and nutmeg.

Set the oven at 400°F (200°C). Knead the dough lightly to knock out the air. Butter the pans, divide the dough in half and set it in the pans. With the oiled back of a spoon or your knuckles, flatten the dough to line the pans. Cover it with the julienne mixture and pour the custard on top. Leave in a warm place to rise 15 minutes. Bake in the preheated oven 40–50 minutes or until the pastry is brown and the custard is set.

Mushroom Bouchées

BOUCHEES AUX CHAMPIGNONS

Although you don't have to work at Chef Jorant's phenomenal speed, try to roll and shape the puff pastry as quickly as possible so the butter won't melt.

For the Puff Pastry Dough:
1½ cups (375 g) unsalted butter
3 cups (375 g) flour
1½ teaspoons (7 g) salt
1½ teaspoons lemon juice—optional
¾–1 cup (2–2.5 dl) ice water
1 egg, beaten to mix with ½ teaspoon salt (for glaze)

For the Filling:
¾ pound (350 g) mushrooms, quartered or diced
Juice of ½ lemon
Salt and pepper
2 cups (5 dl) milk
1 slice of onion
1 bay leaf
6 peppercorns
3 tablespoons (45 g) butter
5 tablespoons (40 g) flour
Pinch of grated nutmeg
3 egg yolks
½ cup (1.25 dl) heavy cream

3½" (9 cm) fluted cookie cutter
2½" (6 cm) fluted or plain cutter

The recipe serves 8 as an appetizer.

Make the puff pastry dough (see **Cocktail Puff Pastries**) and chill. Set the oven at 425°F (220°C). Dampen a baking sheet.

For the bouchées: Stamp out 16 rounds with the large cutter. Turn over and transfer 8 of them to the baking sheet. Brush with egg glaze, taking care that it does not drip onto the sheet. With the smaller cutter cut a circle from the center of the remaining rounds. Turn over and set the resulting rings on top of the rounds on the baking sheet, pressing gently to seal. Brush the rings with glaze and chill 15 minutes. Bake in the heated oven 15–20 minutes or until puffed and brown. Transfer to a rack to cool; while still warm, lift out the "hat" and scoop out any uncooked dough. The bouchées can be kept 1–2 days in an airtight container, or they can be frozen.

For the filling: Put the mushrooms in a saucepan with lemon juice, salt, pepper and a spoonful or two of water. Cover and cook over high heat 4–5 minutes or until the liquid boils up to the top of the pan. Let cool; then drain, reserving the liquid. Scald the milk. Add the onion, bay leaf and peppercorns and let infuse 5–10 minutes. In a heavy-based saucepan melt the butter, whisk in the flour and cook 1–2 minutes until foaming but not browned; let cool. Strain in the hot milk and mushroom liquid, whisk well; then bring to a boil, whisking constantly. Add salt, pepper and nutmeg to taste and simmer 3–5 minutes to a thick coating consistency. Add the mushrooms and taste for seasoning. The filling can be made up to 48 hours ahead and kept covered in the refrigerator.

To finish: Reheat the bouchées in a 250°F (120°C) oven. Reheat the filling. Mix the yolks and cream in a bowl, stir in a little of the hot sauce and stir this mixture back into remaining sauce. Heat until it thickens slightly but do not boil. Taste for seasoning and keep hot, if necessary, in a water bath. Just before serving, fill the bouchées with the mushroom mixture, mounding it well, and top with a "hat."

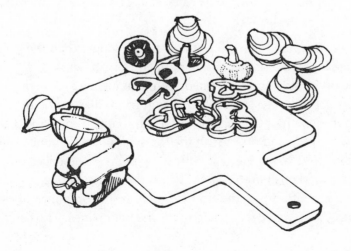

Sea Bass in Pastry
LOUP EN CROUTE

As with puff pastry, roll out the brioche and decorate the fish quickly to prevent the butter in the dough from melting. Chef Jorant says his cold hands are an advantage, and during hot weather when they're warmer than usual, he sometimes plunges them into ice water to lower their temperature.

Brioche dough (see **Brioches**)
4–5 pound (2–2.5 kg) whole sea bass, scaled and cleaned, with the head on
1–2 tablespoons oil (for brushing)
1 egg, beaten to mix with ½ teaspoon salt (for glaze)
Salt and pepper
Fresh herbs—thyme, basil, parsley

For the Hollandaise Sauce:
¾ cup (180 g) butter
3 tablespoons water
3 egg yolks
Salt and white pepper
Juice of ½ lemon, or to taste

The fish serves 6–8.

Make the brioche dough and chill at least 4 hours or overnight. Wash the bass and dry thoroughly, inside and out. Cut off the fins and trim the tail to a "V." Cut a paper pattern the same shape and a little larger than the bass. Butter a baking sheet.

Divide the dough in half, roll out half a little longer than the length of the fish and set it on the prepared baking sheet. Brush with oil, set the fish on top lying on its side and trim the dough, leaving a 1″ (2.5 cm) border. Brush the border with egg glaze. Add dough trimmings to the remainder, roll it out to the length of the fish and cut a fish shape, using paper pattern. Season the fish inside and out, brush the top with oil, set a bunch of herbs in the stomach and cover the fish with dough. Press the edges of dough together to seal and push in to neaten. Brush the dough with egg glaze and decorate the fish with a mouth and eye made from trimmings of dough. Snip with scissors to make scales and mark the tail in lines. The fish can be kept, tightly covered with plastic wrap, overnight in the refrigerator, or it can be frozen.

For the hollandaise sauce: Melt the butter, skim froth from the surface and let cool to tepid. In a small saucepan, whisk the water and egg yolks with a little salt and pepper. Set over low heat or in a water bath and whisk constantly until creamy and thick enough for the whisk to leave a trail on the base of the pan. The base of the pan should never be more than hand-hot. Take from the heat and whisk in the butter, a few drops at a time. When the sauce has started to thicken, the butter can be added a little faster. Do not add the milky sediment at the bottom of the butter. Add salt, pepper and lemon juice to taste. The sauce is served warm, not hot; keep warm in a water bath to avoid curdling.

To finish: Set the oven at 425°F (220°C). Let the brioche rise in a warm place 30–45 minutes or until slightly puffed. Bake in the preheated oven 10 minutes, turn down the oven to 375°F (190°C) and bake 30–35 more minutes or until a skewer inserted in the center for 30 seconds is hot to the touch when withdrawn. Transfer the fish to a large platter and serve hollandaise sauce separately. *At the table:* Cut around the edge of the fish to loosen the crust and lift it off to disclose the fish. Carve the fish from the bone as usual and serve a piece of brioche with each portion.

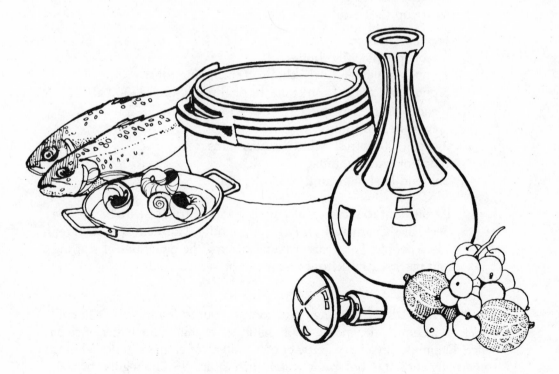

Braised Ham with Spinach in Pastry

JAMBON BRAISE AUX EPINARDS EN CROUTE

As the pastry bakes, it often browns too quickly. Chef Jorant puts a "hat" of foil over the top, and notes: "The pastry is just like me—I have to put on a hat when I'm out in the sun".

14–16 pound (6–7 kg) whole ham
2 tablespoons oil
2 onions, quartered
2 carrots, quartered
2 cloves garlic, crushed
Bouquet garni
3 cups (7.5 dl) stock
2 cups (5 dl) white wine
Freshly ground black pepper
1 egg, beaten to mix with ½ teaspoon salt (for glaze)

For the Pie Pastry:
6 cups (750 g) flour
2 cups (375 g) unsalted butter
6 egg yolks
3 teaspoons (15 g) salt
¾–1 cup (2–2.5 dl) cold water

For the Stuffing:
6 tablespoons (90 g) butter
1 bunch scallions, finely chopped (including tops)
3 pounds (1.5 kg) fresh spinach, or three 10-ounce (300 g)
  packages frozen spinach, cooked and chopped
3 eggs, beaten to mix
2 cups (100 g) fresh white breadcrumbs
Pinch of grated nutmeg
Salt and freshly ground black pepper

If you want to serve a sauce with the ham, try Madeira Sauce (see **Beef Fillet Cherniavsky**). A 14-16 pound (6-7 kg) ham is enough for 14-16 people. For a larger ham, increase the quantities of stuffing and pastry. Any leftover ham can be served cold.

Three days ahead: If using an uncooked country ham, soak it in cold water 12–24 hours, depending on its saltiness, changing the water once or twice. Drain, put in a large kettle of cold water, cover and simmer 3 hours to partially cook it. Cool in the water, then drain. If using regular or processed ham, no boiling is necessary.

One or two days ahead, braise the ham: Set the oven at 350°F (175°C). Remove any skin and all but a thin layer of fat from the ham. In a large roasting pan, heat the oil and brown the ham on all sides. Take it out, add the onions and carrots and cook 5–7 minutes over low heat until soft but not brown. Replace the ham and add the garlic, bouquet garni, stock, wine and pepper (no salt is needed as ham is salty). Cover, bring to a boil and braise in the oven 2–2½ hours or until tender when pierced with a skewer. Let the ham cool, then chill it. If the liquid is not too salty, it can be used to make Madeira sauce.

Make the pie pastry dough (see **Normandy Pear Pie**) and chill 30 minutes. *For the stuffing:* Heat the butter and cook the scallions slowly until soft but not brown. Add chopped spinach and cook over low heat until dry. Remove from the heat and, while still warm, stir in the eggs. Add the breadcrumbs, nutmeg, salt and pepper to taste and leave to cool.

Set the ham on a carving board with the shank bone towards you. With a long thin knife, slice horizontally across the top of the ham. When the slices become large, cut them in half. When the shank bone is reached, angle the knife to cut slices on each side but leave a firm base of uncut ham. Reshape the ham by spreading each slice with a little stuffing, then replacing the slices in their original position.

To wrap the ham in pastry: Reserve a quarter of the dough for decoration. Roll out the remaining dough to an 18″ (45 cm) square. Brush a 2″ (5 cm) border of egg glaze on the edges of dough, roll it around a rolling pin, lift and unroll over the ham, glazed side down, so two points are at each end of ham. Wrap the points under the ham so it is completely covered with dough and press lightly to seal. Trim dough from the shank bone so it is exposed. Brush the dough all over with glaze.

To decorate: Roll out the remaining dough ¼″ (6 mm) thick and cut three 12″ (30 cm) strips. Twist the strips and arrange in an oval around the edge of the top half of the ham, pressing to seal them to the pastry. This oval forms a "lid" for serving. Cut decorations from the remaining dough, arrange on the "lid" and brush them carefully with glaze. Chill at least 30 minutes or until the dough is very firm. The ham can be prepared up to 24 hours ahead and kept covered in the refrigerator.

To finish: Set the oven at 425°F (220°C). Bake the ham 10–15 minutes or until browned, then turn the oven down to 350°F (175°C) and continue to bake 1–1½ hours or until a meat thermometer inserted in the center of the ham registers 160°F (70°C). If the pastry gets very brown, cover it loosely with foil.

To serve: Transfer the ham to a platter. Loosen the "lid" just outside the twisted pastry edge. Fit a paper frill on the shank bone. At the table, lift off the lid, cut in pieces and serve with the ham slices.

Lamb Chops in Puff Pastry

COTELETTES D'AGNEAU EN CUIRASSE

Be sure that all ingredients to be wrapped in puff pastry are completely cool; chill them if possible. Glaze the dough evenly, without letting any glaze drip on the baking sheet, which would prevent the dough from rising properly. The chef compares glaze to paint: "Always brush on two layers of it, to get an even coat."

8 rib lamb chops
2 tablespoons oil
Salt and freshly ground black pepper
8 slices cooked ham
1 egg, beaten to mix with ½ teaspoon salt (for glaze)

For the Puff Pastry Dough:
1½ cups (375 g) unsalted butter
3 cups (375 g) flour
1½ teaspoons (7 g) salt
1½ teaspoons lemon juice—optional
¾–1 cup (2–2.5 dl) ice water

For the Duxelles:
½ onion, finely chopped
2 tablespoons (30 g) butter
½ pound (250 g) mushrooms, finely chopped
½ garlic clove, crushed—optional
1 tablespoon chopped parsley
Salt and freshly ground black pepper

*2½–3" (6–7.5 cm) plain and ½–¾" (1.25–2 cm) fluted
  cookie cutters*
Pastry wheel

For this recipe it is important that the butcher cut the chops so each one has a rib bone.

Make the dough (see **Cocktail Puff Pastries**) and chill. Trim the fat and meat from the ends of the chops to expose about 1" (2.5 cm) of bone; scrape the bone ends clean. In a skillet heat the oil and brown the chops over high heat, allowing 30 seconds on each side. Season and leave to cool. Cut sixteen rounds of ham the same size as the chops.

For the duxelles: In a skillet cook the onion slowly in the butter until soft but not brown. Add the mushrooms and cook over high heat, stirring, until all the moisture has evaporated. Add the garlic and cook 30 seconds longer. Stir in the chopped parsley with salt and pepper to taste and let cool.

Roll out the dough to a 16–18″ (40–45 cm) rectangle and cut in half crosswise. Brush half with beaten egg glaze and set eight rounds of ham on top in two parallel lines, ¾–1″ (2–2.5 cm) from the edge. Spread each round with duxelles, using half the mixture, and top with a chop, arranging the chops so their bones protrude over the edge of the dough. Spread the remaining duxelles on the chops and top with rounds of ham. Cover the chops with the second sheet of dough, letting it fall loosely down between them. NOTE: do not stretch it. Using a ball of dough dipped in flour, press it down firmly to seal the layers of dough around the chops. Cut around each chop with a pastry wheel, leaving a ½″ (1.25 cm) border; press the edges to seal. Brush with egg glaze and set on a dampened baking sheet.

Pile the dough trimmings one on top of another and roll out in a thin layer. Cut eight ¼″ (6 mm) strips, twist them and arrange one around the edge of each chop. Cut twenty-four rounds with the fluted cutter and set three on each chop. Brush the decorations with egg glaze, make a hole in the center with the point of a knife to allow steam to escape and chill the chops 15 minutes. They can be prepared up to 6 hours ahead and kept covered in the refrigerator.

To finish: Set the oven at 425°F (220°C). Bake the chops until puffed and brown, allowing 12–15 minutes for medium rare and 15–18 minutes for well done. Arrange on a platter, bones pointing up and outwards, put chop frills on the bones and serve at once.

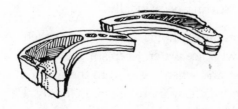

Coffee Bavarian Cream
BAVAROIS AU CAFE

Be especially careful to add the dissolved gelatin to hot custard. Once when a student couldn't understand why his Bavarian cream fell apart, the chef actually pulled pieces of gelatin from the mixture. The gelatin had been added to cool custard and was never completely incorporated.

2 cups (5 dl) milk
1 vanilla bean
1 envelope (¼ ounce or 7 g) gelatin
¼ cup (6 cl) cold water
2½–3 teaspoons dry instant coffee
6 egg yolks
6 tablespoons (90 g) sugar
½ cup (1.25 dl) heavy cream

For Decoration:
½ cup (1.25 dl) heavy cream
2 teaspoons sugar
½ teaspoon vanilla extract

3–4 cups (7.5 dl–1 L) plain mold
Pastry bag with medium star tube

Scald the milk with the vanilla bean, cover and leave to infuse 10–15 minutes. Sprinkle the gelatin over the water in a small bowl and leave 5 minutes or until spongy. Rinse the mold with cold water.

Reheat the milk to boiling with the coffee. Beat the yolks with the sugar until thick and light. Whisk in half the hot milk and whisk the mixture back into the remaining milk. Heat gently, stirring constantly with a wooden spoon, until the custard thickens slightly; if you draw a finger across the back of the spoon, it will leave a clear trail. NOTE: do not over-cook or it will curdle. Take from heat at once and strain into a metal bowl. Add the softened gelatin to the hot custard, stir until completely dissolved and leave to cool, stirring occasionally.

Whip the cream until it holds a soft shape. When cool, set the custard mixture over a bowl of ice water. Keep stirring the mixture; when you feel it becoming thicker and when it is cold to the touch, it is beginning to set. Now add the whipped cream by folding it in lightly. Pour the mixture into the prepared mold. Cover and leave in the refrigerator 1–2 hours or until firmly set. The dessert can be made up to 24 hours ahead, but it tends to stiffen and must be brought to room temperature before serving.

Not more than 3 hours before serving, unmold the dessert: Run a knife around the edge, pull the mixture away from the mold with a finger to release the airlock and dip the bottom of the mold in a bowl of hot water for a few seconds. Set a platter upside down on top and turn over the mold and platter. Give a sharp shake so the dessert falls onto the platter.

For decoration: In a chilled bowl whip the cream until it starts to thicken. Add the sugar and vanilla and continue beating until the cream holds peaks. Using a pastry bag fitted with a medium star tube, decorate the edge of the Bavarian cream with rosettes of whipped cream. Keep in the refrigerator until ready to serve.

Chocolate Charlotte
CHARLOTTE AU CHOCOLAT

"Always whistle when adding rum or other alcohol to a mixture," says Chef Jorant, "so your boss knows you're not drinking it!"

12–15 ladyfingers (see **Ladyfingers**)
1 envelope (¼ ounce or 7 g) gelatin
¼ cup (6 cl) water
6 ounces (180 g) semisweet chocolate, chopped
2 cups (5 dl) milk
2 teaspoons dry instant coffee
5 egg yolks
¼ cup (60 g) sugar
½ cup (1.25 dl) heavy cream
1 tablespoon rum

For Decoration:
3–4 ounces (90–120 g) semisweet chocolate, chopped
¾ cup (2 dl) heavy cream
1–2 teaspoons sugar
1 teaspoon rum

Charlotte mold (1½ quart or 1.5 L capacity)
Pastry bag with medium star tube

Line the base of the charlotte mold with a circle of waxed paper. Line the sides of the mold with ladyfingers, trimming them so they fit tightly.

Sprinkle the gelatin over the water in a small bowl and leave 5 minutes or until spongy. Melt 6 ounces (180 g) chocolate in a heatproof bowl over a pan of hot water.

Bring the milk and coffee to a boil. Meanwhile beat the egg yolks with the sugar until thick and light. Whisk in the hot milk and return this custard mixture to the pan. Heat, stirring constantly, until the custard thickens slightly. Do not boil or it will curdle. Take from the heat and stir in the softened gelatin until melted. Slowly stir the custard into the melted chocolate and leave to cool, stirring occasionally. Whip the cream.

When the custard is cool, add the rum, set the bowl over ice and stir until the mixture starts to set. Fold in the whipped cream and pour the mixture into the lined charlotte mold. NOTE: the mixture must be fairly thick or it will soak the ladyfingers. Cover and chill at least 2 hours or until set. The charlotte can be made a day ahead and kept in the refrigerator but the gelatin mixture tends to stiffen, so let it stand 1–2 hours at room temperature before serving.

For decoration: Melt the chopped chocolate in a heatproof bowl over a pan of hot water. For squares, spread chocolate evenly about 1/8 ″ (3 mm) thick over an 8″ (20 cm) waxed paper square and, when on the point of setting, mark into squares with a sharp knife. For rounds, cut waxed paper into 1–1½ ″ (about 3–4 cm) circles and spread them with chocolate. Chill until set; then peel away the paper.

To finish: In a chilled bowl whip the cream until it starts to thicken. Add the sugar and rum and continue beating until the cream holds a shape and sticks to the whisk. Trim the ladyfingers level with the top of the charlotte and unmold it onto a platter. Use the pastry bag and star tube to decorate the base with rosettes of whipped cream, and top them with chocolate squares or rounds. Chill until ready to serve.

Almond Petits Fours
PETITS FOURS AUX AMANDES

In just a few minutes, Chef Jorant pipes enough petits fours to cover several baking sheets. The cookies of each shape should be as uniform as possible so they bake evenly and an attractive platter can be arranged. Chef Jorant is even careful to cut all pieces of candied fruit for decoration to exactly the same size.

1½ cups (200 g) whole blanched almonds, peeled and ground
¾ cup (150 g) sugar
1 teaspoon apricot jam—optional
2 egg whites, beaten to mix
½ teaspoon vanilla extract

For Decoration, one or more of the following:
Blanched almonds, split in half
Candied cherries or candied orange peel, cut in pieces
Small diamonds of angelica
Raisins

For the Glaze:
1 tablespoon confectioners' sugar
2 tablespoons milk or water

Parchment paper
Pastry bag with large star tube

The recipe makes 12–14 petits fours.

Line a baking sheet with parchment paper. Set the oven at 350°F (175°C).

Mix the ground almonds and sugar, add apricot jam and stir in enough egg white to make a mixture that is soft enough to pipe but still holds its shape. Beat in vanilla. Using a pastry bag fitted with a large star tube, pipe the mixture in flowers, rosettes or figure eights onto the prepared baking sheet. Decorate with split almonds, pieces of cherry or orange peel, angelica or raisins and bake 15–20 minutes or until they begin to brown. Leave on the baking sheet.

For the glaze: Heat the sugar with the milk until dissolved and brush over the petits fours while still hot. Lift one end of the paper slightly, immediately pour a glass of water under the paper and stand back. NOTE: the hot baking sheet will turn the water into steam, making it easy to remove the petits fours. Leave them for a few moments; then remove from the paper and transfer to a rack to cool. They can be stored 1–2 weeks in an airtight container, or they can be frozen.

Russian Cigarettes

CIGARETTES RUSSES

"That's not a cigarette; it's a Havana cigar!" Chef Jorant admonishes stu dents who make these cookies too big.

⅔ cup (250 g) confectioners' sugar, sifted
6 egg whites (about 1 cup or 2.5 dl)
1¼ cups (150 g) flour
1 tablespoon heavy cream
1 teaspoon vanilla extract

Pastry bag with ⅜ " (1 cm) plain tube

The recipe makes about 40 cigarettes.

Grease 2 or 3 baking sheets and preheat the oven to 450°F (230°C).

Cream the butter and confectioners' sugar and gradually beat in half of the egg whites. Beat until the ingredients are well mixed. Add 1 heaping teaspoon flour and mix well. Gradually beat in the remaining egg whites. Stir in the remaining flour; then add the heavy cream and vanilla and mix well. Using a pastry bag fitted with the plain tube, pipe mounds the size of walnuts well apart on the prepared baking sheets. Tap the baking sheets sharply on a table to flatten the mounds and bake 4–5 minutes or until brown around the edges.

Loosen the cookies from the baking sheets with a sharp pliable knife or metal spatula but do not remove them. One by one, put a cookie upside down on a table, roll quickly around a wooden spoon handle or pencil and press hard to seal. Remove the cookie at once and leave on a rack to cool. Roll each remaining cookie as quickly as possible. If they become too hard to roll, return to the oven for 1 minute to soften. NOTE: as a precaution, pipe and bake one test cigarette first. If it is not crisp when rolled and cooled, add 1 tablespoon (15 g) melted butter to the mixture. If it is too brittle, add 1–2 tablespoons more flour.

The cookies can be stored in an airtight container for up to a week.

Raisin Cookies
PALETS DE DAMES

Chef Jorant warns agains putting too much salt in sweet pastries. In his own pastry shop, he taught his apprentices not to put any salt in this type of cookie.

¼ cup (30 g) currants or raisins
⅔ cup (100 g) flour
Tiny pinch of salt—optional
7 tablespoons (100 g) butter
½ cup (100 g) sugar
2 egg whites, beaten to mix
½ teaspoon vanilla extract

Pastry bag with ⅜ " (1 cm) plain tube

The recipe makes 2 dozen cookies.

Set the oven at 400°F (200°C) and grease and flour two baking sheets. Pour boiling water over the currants or raisins; let stand 10 minutes or until plump; then drain and dry well on paper towels. Sift the flour with the salt.

Cream the butter, beat in the sugar and continue beating until light and fluffy. Beat in the egg whites a little at a time, beating well after each addition. Stir in the vanilla; then fold in the flour. With a pastry bag fitted with the plain tube, pipe 1" (2.5 cm) mounds onto the prepared sheets, leaving plenty of room for spreading. Put 2–3 currants or raisins on each mound.

Bake 8–10 minutes or until the edges are golden but the centers are still pale. Transfer to a rack to cool. The cookies can be kept in an airtight container for 3–4 days.

Florentines
FLORENTINES

Because chocolate is sensitive to heat and will often be dull rather than glossy if overheated, melt it over hot but not boiling water, never over direct heat.

3 tablespoons (45 g) butter
½ cup (1.25 dl) heavy cream
⅔ cup (125 g) sugar
¼ cup (30 g) candied cherries, soaked in hot water, drained and quartered
1¼ cups (150 g) blanched almonds, finely chopped
½ cup (50 g) shredded almonds
¾ cup (100 g) candied orange peel, finely chopped
⅓ cup (50 g) flour
8 ounces (250 g) semisweet chocolate, chopped (for coating)

3" (7.5 cm) plain cookie cutter
Cake decorating comb—optional

The recipe makes about 30 florentines.

Grease and lightly flour two baking sheets and set the oven at 350°F (175°C).

Bring the butter, cream and sugar slowly to a boil. Take from the heat and stir in the cherries, chopped and shredded almonds, candied peel and flour. Drop teaspoonsful of the mixture onto the prepared baking sheets, leaving plenty of room for spreading, and flatten each with a wet fork.

Bake 5–6 minutes. Take from the oven and, with a cookie cutter, pull in the edges of each cookie. Return to the oven and bake 5–6 minutes longer or until lightly browned at the edges. Cool a little on the baking sheets; then lift off with a sharp knife and transfer to a rack.

Melt the chocolate on a heatproof plate over a pan of hot water. Stir with a wooden spoon until smooth and thick. Spread the smooth undersides of the cookies with chocolate and, if you like, when on the point of setting, mark it with wavy lines using a cake decorating comb or a large serrated knife.

Ladyfingers
BISCUITS A LA CUILLER

Making good ladyfingers takes practice, but in any case your own will be better than those you can buy. Handle the delicate mixture carefully, especially when folding and piping.

> ⅔ cup (100 g) flour
> Tiny pinch of salt
> 4 eggs, separated
> ½ cup (100 g) sugar
> ½ teaspoon vanilla extract—optional
> Confectioners' sugar (for sprinkling)
>
> *Pastry bag with large plain tube*
>
> The recipe makes about 30 ladyfingers.

Set the oven at 300°F (150°C). Cover a baking sheet with parchment paper or grease and flour it lightly.

Sift the flour and salt together twice. Beat the egg yolks with half the sugar and the vanilla until light and thick enough to leave a ribbon trail. Whip the egg whites until stiff, add the remaining sugar and beat 20 seconds longer or until glossy. Pour the sifted flour over the yolks. Add about one-quarter of the egg whites to the yolk mixture and fold together with the flour as lightly as possible. Gently fold in the remaining egg whites in two batches. NOTE: the mixture must be folded as quickly as possible but with great care as it must remain stiff enough to pipe.

Gently spoon the mixture into a pastry bag fitted with a large plain tube and pipe fingers about 3½″ (9 cm) long and 1″ (2.5 cm) apart on the prepared baking sheet. Immediately sprinkle the tops with confectioners' sugar, gently shake off the excess sugar and bake in preheated oven, with the door held slightly ajar by a wooden spoon, 15–18 minutes or until light beige, firm on the outside and still soft in the center. Transfer to a rack to cool.

Strawberry Mousse Cake
GENOISE A LA MOUSSE DE FRAISES

"It practically slices itself," declares Chef Jorant as he quickly divides a cake into very thin and perfectly even layers. The secret is a long serrated knife and a light sawing motion.

For the Genoise:
¾ cup (100 g) flour
Tiny pinch of salt
¼ cup (60 g) butter
⅔ cup (125 g) sugar
4 eggs
½ teaspoon vanilla extract

For the Filling and Frosting:
1½ envelopes (⅓ ounce or 10 g) gelatin
7 tablespoons water
½ pint (250 g) strawberries
9 tablespoons (115 g) sugar
1½ cups (3.75 dl) heavy cream
1 teaspoon vanilla extract
5–6 strawberries (for decoration)

10" (25 cm) layer pan, or 9" (23 cm) springform pan
Pastry bag with medium star tube

The genoise proportions are for American all-purpose flour. The cake serves 8.

Set the oven at 350°F (175°C). Prepare the cake pan and make the genoise mixture (see **Singapore Cake**). Bake in the preheated oven 35–40 minutes or until the mixture springs back when lightly pressed with a fingertip. Run a knife around the edge of the cake and turn it out onto a rack to cool. The cake can be made ahead and kept in an airtight container 2–3 days, or it can be frozen.

For the strawberry mousse filling: Sprinkle the gelatin over ¼ cup (6 cl) water in a small bowl and leave 5 minutes or until spongy. Purée the strawberries in a blender or food processor or work through a strainer. Make syrup by bringing ½ cup (100 g) sugar and 3 tablespoons water just to a boil. Add the softened gelatin to the hot syrup, stir until melted and leave to cool, stirring occasionally. Stir in strawberry purée. In a chilled bowl whip the cream until it starts to thicken. Add remaining sugar and vanilla and continue beating until the cream forms soft peaks and sticks to the whisk. Set the strawberry mixture in a bowl of ice water and stir until it starts to thicken. Fold in one-third of the whipped cream and remove the mixture from the bowl of ice water. When the mousse is on the point of setting, it must be immediately spread on the genoise or it will set.

To assemble: Split the genoise in three layers and sandwich them with the mousse. Spread more mousse on top. Spread whipped cream on the sides. Decorate the cake with rosettes of whipped cream, using a pastry bag fitted with a medium star tube. Top each rosette with a strawberry.

Singapore Cake
GATEAU SINGAPOUR

If using a powerful electric mixer to make the genoise, you need not heat the egg and sugar mixture.

For the Genoise:
½ cup (75 g) flour
Tiny pinch of salt
3 tablespoons (45 g) unsalted butter
½ cup (100 g) sugar
3 eggs
½ teaspoon vanilla extract

For the Filling and Frosting:
1 can (1 pound or 500 g) pineapple rings
3–4 tablespoons kirsch, or to taste
1 tablespoon apricot jam
3 egg yolks
6 tablespoons (90 g) sugar
3 tablespoons water
¾ cup (180 g) unsalted butter

For the Syrup:
½ cup (100 g) sugar
⅓ cup (1 dl) water
1 tablespoon kirsch

For Decoration:
1 pineapple ring
3–4 candied cherries
Angelica leaves or hazelnuts—optional

9″ (23 cm) layer pan, or 8″ (20 cm) springform pan

The genoise proportions are for American all-purpose flour. The cake serves 6.

Brush the cake pan with melted butter, leave for a few minutes, then sprinkle with flour, discarding the excess. Set the oven at 350°F (175°C).

For the genoise: Sift the flour with the salt 2–3 times. Clarify the butter. In a large bowl gradually beat the sugar into the eggs. Set the bowl over a pan of hot water and beat 8–10 minutes or until mixture is light and thick enough to leave a ribbon trail when the whisk is lifted. Take from the heat, add the vanilla and continue beating until the mixture is cool.

Sift the flour over the batter in three batches, folding in each as lightly as possible and adding the butter with the last batch. Pour into the prepared cake pan and bake in the preheated oven 25–30 minutes or until the cake shrinks slightly from the sides of the pan and the top springs back when lightly pressed with a fingertip. Run a knife around the edge of the cake and turn it out onto a rack to cool. The cake can be baked ahead and kept in an airtight container 2–3 days, or it can be frozen.

For the filling: Save one pineapple ring for decoration and chop the rest until very fine. Mix with 1 tablespoon kirsch and apricot jam. *For the butter cream:* In a bowl beat the egg yolks until light. Heat the sugar with the water until dissolved and boil until this syrup reaches the soft ball stage (239°F or 115°C; a teaspoonful of syrup dipped carefully in cold water forms a soft ball). Gradually pour the hot syrup onto the yolks, beating constantly, and continue beating until cool and thick. Cream the butter and gradually beat it into the yolk mixture. Beat in 2–3 tablespoons kirsch to taste.

For the syrup: In a saucepan, heat the sugar and water and boil 1–2 minutes or until the syrup is clear. Remove from the heat and add the kirsh.

To finish the cake: Split the genoise, brush each layer with kirsch-flavored syrup and spread with butter cream. Spoon some chopped pineapple onto each layer. Assemble the cake and coat the top and sides with the remaining butter cream.

For decoration: Cut the reserved pineapple ring into 5 or 6 wedges and arrange them in a star on top of the cake, with the narrow section of each wedge pointing outwards. Halve each candied cherry and place half a cherry at the top of each wedge. If you like, decorate with a few angelica leaves or hazelnuts.

Rolled Sponge Cake with Chocolate Filling
GENOISE ROULE A LA GANACHE

Chef Jorant sometimes makes twice the amount of chocolate ganache and uses it both for filling and for frosting. A double-rich result.

For the Cake:
5 tablespoons (40 g) flour
¼ cup (35 g) cornstarch
3 eggs
3 egg yolks
⅓ cup (80 g) sugar
½ teaspoon vanilla extract
Confectioners' sugar (for sprinkling)

For the Ganache Chocolate Filling:
⅓ cup (1 dl) heavy cream
4 ounces (125 g) semisweet chocolate, chopped

The cake serves 6–8.

Grease a sheet of parchment paper and set it on a large baking sheet. Set the oven at 375°F (190°C).

For the cake: Sift the flour with the cornstarch. Whisk the eggs, yolks and sugar in a bowl until mixed. Set the bowl over a pan of hot but not boiling water and whisk until the mixture is light and fluffy and leaves a ribbon trail when the whisk is lifted. Take from the heat and continue beating until cool. Stir in the vanilla; then fold in the flour as lightly as possible, in two or three batches. Spread the mixture on the prepared baking sheet to a very thin rectangle about 16"x20" (40x50 cm). Bake in preheated oven 10–12 minutes or until very lightly browned. NOTE: do not overcook the cake or it will crack. Take the cake from the oven and at once cover with a dish towel to prevent steam escaping. This ensures that the cake can be rolled without cracking. Leave to cool; then turn the cake, with the dish towel, onto a rack and peel off the paper.

For the filling: Scald the cream. Take from the heat, add the chocolate and stir until melted. Leave to cool; then beat 5 minutes so the filling is light and very smooth.

Trim the edges of the cake, spread it with the filling and roll it, using the dish towel. Trim the ends diagonally, sprinkle the roll with confectioners' sugar and transfer to a platter for serving. The cake is best eaten the day it is made, or it can be frozen.

Almond Meringue Cake
GATEAU PROGRES

Chef Jorant removes the baking sheet of meringue from the oven with his bare hands—a trick to be watched rather than copied!

For the Meringue Layers:
1 cup (125 g) shelled hazelnuts
1 cup (125 g) whole blanched almonds, peeled
8 egg whites
1¼ cups (250 g) sugar
½ teaspoon vanilla extract

For the Praline Butter Cream:
Praline (see **Gâteau Paris-Brest**)
4 egg yolks
½ cup (125 g) sugar
¼ cup (6 cl) water
1 cup (250 g) unsalted butter

For Finish:
Confectioners' sugar (for sprinkling)
¾ cup (100 g) blanched almonds, peeled, browned and chopped

Pastry bag with ⅜" (1 cm) plain tube
Paper piping cone

If you like, flavor the praline butter cream with coffee or chocolate by adding either 2–3 teaspoons dry instant coffee dissolved in 1 tablespoon hot water or 3 ounces (90 g) melted semisweet chocolate. The recipe makes two cakes.

For the meringue layers: Toast the hazelnuts and whole blanched almonds in a 350°F (175°C) oven 8–12 minutes or until browned. Let cool slightly, then rub the hazelnuts with a rough cloth or against a sieve to remove the skins. In a blender, electric food mill or rotary cheese grater, grind the almonds and hazelnuts to a powder, a little at a time. Grease and flour two baking sheets and mark three 9" (23 cm) circles on each with a pan lid. Turn the oven to 250°F (120°C).

Whip the egg whites until stiff. Beat in 2 tablespoons (30 g) of the sugar until the whites are glossy; then fold in the remaining sugar. Fold in the browned ground nuts with the vanilla. Pipe in 9" (23 cm) rounds on the prepared baking sheets and bake in the preheated oven 40–50 minutes or until crisp, dry and just beginning to brown. Trim the rounds neatly with a sharp knife while still hot, then transfer to a rack to cool. They can be kept up to two weeks in an airtight container.

For the filling: Make the praline and grind to a powder. Make the butter cream: In a bowl beat the egg yolks lightly. Heat the sugar with the water until dissolved and boil until the syrup reaches the soft ball stage (239°F or 115°C on a sugar thermometer; a teaspoonful of syrup dipped carefully in cold water forms a soft ball). Gradually pour the hot syrup onto the yolks, beating constantly, and continue beating until cool and thick. Cream the butter and gradually beat it into the yolk mixture. Beat in the praline.

To assemble: Sandwich the meringue layers with about two-thirds of the butter cream. Spread more butter cream on the top and sides, reserving 2–3 tablespoons. Sprinkle the top of the cake generously with confectioners' sugar and press browned chopped almonds around the sides with a metal spatula. Put the reserved butter cream frosting in a paper piping cone and pipe the word "Progrès" across the top of the cake. The cake should be assembled one day ahead so the flavor will mellow and the cake will be easier to slice. It keeps well in the refrigerator 2–3 days, and it can be frozen.

Cream Puffs with Chocolate Sauce
PROFITEROLES AU CHOCOLAT

Among favorite French desserts, profiteroles must be second only to chocolate mousse. These could also be filled with vanilla ice cream.

Choux pastry (see **Caramel Glazed Puffs**)
1 egg, beaten with ½ teaspoon salt (for glaze)

For the Filling:
6 egg yolks
½ cup (125 g) sugar
6 tablespoons (50 g) flour
2 cups (5 dl) milk
1 vanilla bean
9 tablespoons (1.5 dl) heavy cream
2 tablespoons confectioners' sugar

For the Chocolate Sauce:
3 ounces (90 g) semisweet chocolate
2 tablespoons (30 g) butter
5 tablespoons water
1 tablespoon rum, brandy or Grand Marnier

Pastry bag; ³⁄₈" (1 cm) and ¼" (6 mm) plain tubes

Set the oven at 400°F (200°C). Prepare the choux pastry. Using a pastry bag fitted with a ³⁄₈" (1 cm) plain tube, pipe 1½" (about 4 cm) mounds of dough well apart onto a baking sheet. Brush with egg glaze. NOTE: if using an unventilated electric oven, prop open the door slightly. Bake in preheated oven 20–25 minutes or until the puffs are firm and brown. Test by removing one puff from the oven and cooling it to be sure it is crisp. Transfer the puffs to a rack to cool. While still warm, prick a tiny hole in the bottom of each with a ¼" (6 mm) piping tube to release the steam. The puffs can be kept overnight in an airtight container, but they are at their best when eaten within a few hours of baking.

For the filling: Beat the yolks with the sugar until thick and light. Stir in the flour and enough cold milk to make a smooth paste. Scald the remaining milk, add the vanilla bean, cover and leave to infuse 10–15 minutes. Remove the bean, whisk the boiling milk into the yolk mixture and blend. Return to the pan and whisk over gentle heat until boiling. Cook gently, whisking constantly, 2 minutes or until the mixture thins slightly, showing the flour is completely cooked. Dot with butter to prevent the formation of a skin and let cool completely. Whisk until smooth. Whip the heavy cream with the confectioners' sugar until stiff and fold into the cool mixture. The filling can be made up to 4 hours ahead and kept in the refrigerator.

For the chocolate sauce: Melt the chocolate and butter in the water over low heat, stirring occasionally. Do not boil. Stir in the rum, brandy or Grand Marnier. The sauce can be made up to 24 hours ahead and kept in the refrigerator.

Not more than 2 hours before serving: Using a pastry bag fitted with a ¼" (6 mm) plain tube, pipe the filling into the hole of each puff. *To serve:* Pile the puffs in a pyramid in a serving bowl and pour over the chocolate sauce to coat them.

Gâteau Paris-Brest
GATEAU PARIS-BREST

*The St. Honoré cream filling for Gâteau Paris-Brest is famous for its delicacy and a standard choice for advanced pâtisserie exams in France. For something less taxing, Chef Jorant recommends a praline-flavored butter cream (see **Almond Meringue Cake**).*

For the Choux Pastry Rings:
1 cup (125 g) flour
½ teaspoon (3 g) salt
1 cup (2.5 dl) water
½ cup (125 g) butter
4–5 eggs
1 egg, beaten to mix with ½ teaspoon salt (for glaze)
4 tablespoons sliced almonds (for sprinkling)
Confectioners' sugar (to finish)

For the Praline:
¾ cup (100 g) whole unblanched almonds
½ cup (100 g) sugar

For the St. Honoré Cream:
5 egg yolks
6 tablespoons (90 g) sugar
5 tablespoons (40 g) flour
1½ cups (3.75 dl) milk
5 egg whites
½ envelope (⅛ ounce or 4 g) gelatin—optional

Pastry bag with ⅝" (1.5 cm) plain tube and large star tube

The recipe makes two gâteaux to serve 8-10.

Set the oven at 400°F (200°C). Make the choux pastry dough (see **Caramel Glazed Puffs**). Using a pastry bag fitted with the plain tube, pipe an 8″ (20 cm) ring of dough on a baking sheet, using a pan lid in the center of the ring as a guide. Pipe a second ring of dough inside the first. Brush with egg glaze and score with the back of a fork dipped in water. Pipe another layer of dough on top, on the crack between the first two rings. Shape a second gâteau in the same way. Brush them with glaze, score with the back of a fork and sprinkle with sliced almonds. NOTE: if using an unventilated electric oven, keep the door propped open slightly while baking. Bake in preheated oven 30–35 minutes or until firm and brown. Transfer to a rack to cool. While still warm, split them horizontally with a serrated knife so steam can escape.

For the praline: Put the almonds and sugar in a heavy-based pan and heat gently, stirring occasionally, until the sugar melts and caramelizes. The almonds should pop, showing they are thoroughly toasted. Pour onto an oiled marble or baking sheet and leave until cold and crisp. Grind to a powder in an electric food mill or with a rotary cheese grater; then work through a coarse sieve. NOTE: any lumps in the praline will block up the star tube.

Make the St. Honoré cream as close to serving time as possible. *First make pastry cream:* Beat the yolks with 4 tablespoons (60 g) sugar until thick and light. Stir in the flour and enough cold milk to make a smooth paste. Scald the remaining milk and whisk into the yolk mixture. Return to the pan and whisk over gentle heat until boiling. Cook gently, whisking constantly, 2 minutes or until the mixture thins slightly, showing the flour is completely cooked. Stir in the praline. At the same time, whip the egg whites until stiff and beat in 2 tablespoons (30 g) sugar. If you must make the St. Honoré cream ahead, add the gelatin by softening it in 2 tablespoons cold water, then stirring it into the hot cream. NOTE: if gelatin is added, the pastry cream will not have as fine a texture. While the cream is still very hot, very quickly stir in one-third of the whipped egg whites; then fold the mixture into the remaining whites as lightly and as quickly as possible. NOTE: if the mixture is folded too much it will be too soft to pipe properly. The hot cream must cook the egg whites in order to be of good piping consistency. Although it is preferable to pipe the St. Honoré cream as soon as possible, the cream and the pastry rings can be made 5–6 hours ahead and kept at room temperature. Keep the pastry in an airtight container.

Not more than 2 hours before serving, complete the gâteaux. Using a pastry bag with a large star tube, pipe as generous a filling as possible onto the lower half of the rings. Top with the upper section—the cream should show around the sides. Sprinkle the gâteaux with confectioners' sugar and transfer to a serving platter.

Brioches
BRIOCHES

Chef Jorant shapes small brioches by rolling one ball of dough, then dividing it in two by pressing and rolling with the sides of his hand. It is quite literally a "tour de main" and you may find the method described here easier.

> 4 cups (500 g) flour
> 2½ teaspoons (12 g) salt
> 2 tablespoons (30 g) sugar
> 1 package dry yeast, or 1 cake (15 g) compressed yeast
> 2 tablespoons lukewarm water
> 6–7 eggs
> 1 cup (250 g) unsalted butter
> 1 egg, beaten to mix with ½ teaspoon salt (for glaze)
>
> *15 small brioche pans, or 2 large brioche pans*
>   *(6" or 15 cm diameter)*

The recipe makes fifteen small brioches or two large 6" (15 cm) loaves.

Sift the flour onto a working surface and make a large well in the center. Place the salt and sugar at one side of the well and the crumbled yeast on the other. Using your fingers, dilute the yeast with the lukewarm water, without mixing in the salt or sugar. Mix in about one-eighth of the flour. Let rise 5–10 minutes. Break in six of the eggs and mix with the salt, sugar and yeast mixture. Flick some of the flour over the center mixture so it is covered. Quickly draw in the remaining flour without letting the liquid escape. Pull the dough into large crumbs. If it is dry, beat the last egg and add it. Press the dough firmly together; it should be soft and sticky.

Mix the dough by pinching off a small portion between the thumb and forefinger of each hand and placing these back on the mass of dough. Repeat 5–7 times. Knead the dough by lifting and slapping it on the working surface until very smooth and elastic. Pound the butter to soften it thoroughly. Mix it into the dough with a pinching motion, then knead again briefly with a slapping motion as above.

Transfer to a lightly oiled or floured bowl, turn the dough over, cover with a damp cloth and let rise at room temperature about 2 hours or until nearly doubled in bulk. Fold in three to knock out the air. Cover and let rise again at room temperature until doubled in bulk, or leave overnight in the refrigerator. The dough is easier to handle if chilled.

Butter the brioche pans. Knead the dough lightly to knock out the air and divide it into fifteen pieces (for individual brioches) or in half (for large loaves). Pinch off one-third of each piece of dough and shape both large and small pieces in balls. Set a large ball in the base of each buttered brioche pan, cut a deep cross in the top and crown it with a smaller ball or "head" of dough. NOTE: The heads of brioche often slip sideways or subside into the lower part of the dough. To help prevent this, the shaped brioches should be chilled at least 12 hours and up to 36 hours in the refrigerator, or they can be frozen for up to three weeks.

Let the brioches rise at room temperature, allowing about 30 minutes for small ones or 1–1¼ hours for large loaves, or until the pans are almost full. (Chilled brioches may already have risen sufficiently in the refrigerator.) Set the oven at 425°F (220°C). Brush the risen brioches with glaze and bake in the preheated oven, allowing 15–20 minutes for small brioches or until they are well browned and give a hollow sound when tapped on the bottom. For large loaves, after 15 minutes, turn down the oven heat to 375°F (190°C) and continue baking 30–40 minutes or until they start pulling away from the sides of the pan and give a hollow sound when tapped on the bottom. Cool on a wire rack. Cooked brioches can be kept 2–3 days in an airtight container, or they can be frozen.

Swiss Brioche
BRIOCHE SUISSE

The amount of candied and dried fruit in this recipe may seem large for the amount of dough, but remember that the dough will triple in volume during rising and expand even more in baking.

Brioche dough (see **Brioches**)
2½ cups (300 g) mixed, chopped candied fruits and raisins
  or currants
¼ cup (6 cl) rum or Cointreau
1 egg, beaten with ½ teaspoon salt (for glaze)
⅓ cup (1 dl) apricot jam or red currant jelly glaze (to finish)

For the Frangipane:
⅓ cup (75 g) butter
⅓ cup (75 g) sugar
1 egg, beaten
⅔ cup (75 g) almonds, blanched, peeled and ground
1 teaspoon rum

Two 8–9" (20–23 cm) layer pans

The recipe makes two Swiss brioches.

Make the brioche dough, let rise and refrigerate several hours or overnight so it will be easy to roll out. Add the candied fruits and raisins or currants to the rum or Cointreau and leave to macerate about 30 minutes.

For the frangipane: Cream the butter, gradually beat in the sugar and continue beating until light and soft. Gradually beat in the egg. Stir in the almonds and rum.

For each pan, roll out a 5-ounce (150 g) piece of dough to a thin 10" (25 cm) circle and line the pans. Prick lightly with a fork. Roll out two 6-ounce (180 g) pieces of dough to thin rectangles. Spread each rectangle with a thin layer of frangipane. Drain the fruit and divide between the two rectangles of dough, spooning it evenly onto the layer of frangipane. Roll each rectangle as if it were a jelly roll and slice in ¾" (2 cm) slices. Put the slices in the lined pans, barely touching each other. With a knife trim the dough lining the pans to about 1" (2.5 cm) below the top of the pan. Let rise, covered with a clean towel, 2–3 hours at room temperature. Set the oven at 400°F (200°C).

Carefully brush the brioches with egg glaze and bake in preheated oven 35–45 minutes or until they are golden brown and pull away from the sides of the pan. When cool, brush with melted jam glaze. The brioches can be kept 2–3 days in an airtight container, or they can be frozen.

Sweet Puff Pastries
FEUILLETES SUCRES

Even if your puff pastry is not as beautiful as Chef Jorant's, these puff pastries will always be delicious.

> Puff pastry dough (see **Cocktail Puff Pastries**)
> OR the equivalent in puff pastry trimmings
> Flavorings (see individual recipes below)

Make the puff pastry and chill thoroughly. Shape the pastries according to each recipe. Set on a dampened baking sheet and chill 15 minutes. Set the oven at 425°F (220°C). Bake the pastries 8–12 minutes until puffed and brown. NOTE: watch carefully as they burn very easily. Transfer to a rack to cool. The pastries can be kept a day or two in an airtight container, or they can be frozen, baked or unbaked.

Almond Twists
SACRISTAINS

Roll out prepared dough to a rectangle 10″ (25 cm) wide and trim the edges. Brush with egg glaze, made by beating one egg with ½ teaspoon salt. Sprinkle with ½ cup (50 g) finely chopped or sliced almonds, then with ½ cup (100 g) granulated sugar. Turn the dough over, brush the other side with egg glaze and sprinkle with ½ cup (50 g) more chopped or sliced almonds and ½ cup (100 g) granulated sugar. Cut the dough into two 5″ (12 cm) wide strips, then crosswise into fingers ¾″ (2 cm) wide. Twist them several times and transfer to a dampened baking sheet, pressing the ends down firmly so they do not unroll during baking. Chill and bake as described above. Makes about 36 sacristains.

Butterflies
PAPILLONS

Give the last two turns to the dough on a surface sprinkled with granulated sugar instead of flour. Chill until firm.

Roll out prepared dough to a rectangle 10″ (25 cm) wide and trim the edges. Cut the dough into three strips each about 3″ (7.5 cm) wide. Arrange them one on top of the other. With the handle of a knife make a deep lengthwise crease in the center. With a sharp knife cut into ⅜″ (1 cm) slices. Twist each once and transfer to a dampened baking sheet. Chill and bake as described above. Makes 30–35 papillons.

Gâteau Pithiviers
GATEAU PITHIVIERS

Air conditioning and chilled marble slabs were unknown in pâtisseries when Chef Jorant learned his trade. But his trick of chilling a working surface by leaving a metal tray of ice cubes on it for several minutes makes rolling puff pastry considerably easier.

For the Puff Pastry Dough:
1½ cups (375 g) unsalted butter
3 cups (375 g) flour
1½ teaspoons (7 g) salt
1½ teaspoons lemon juice—optional
¾–1 cup (2–2.5 dl) ice water
1 egg, beaten with ½ teaspoon salt (for glaze)
Granulated or confectioners' sugar (for sprinkling)

For the Frangipane Filling:
½ cup (125 g) butter, softened
⅔ cup (125 g) sugar
1 egg
1 egg yolk
1 cup (125 g) whole blanched almonds, peeled and ground
2 tablespoons (15 g) flour
2 tablespoons rum

The gâteau serves 6–8.

Make the puff pastry dough (see **Cocktail Puff Pastries**) and chill. *For the filling:* Cream the butter in a bowl; add the sugar and beat thoroughly. Beat in the egg and the yolk; then stir in the almonds, flour and rum.

Roll out half the pastry to approximately an 11″ (27 cm) circle. Using a pan lid as a guide, cut out a 10″ (25 cm) circle with a sharp knife, angling the knife slightly. Roll out the remaining dough slightly thicker than the first round and cut another 10″ (25 cm) circle. Set the thin circle on a baking sheet, mound the filling in the center, leaving a 1″ (2.5 cm) border, and brush the border with egg glaze. Set the remaining circle on top, press the edges together firmly and indent them with the back of a knife. Scallop the edge of the gâteau by pulling it in at intervals with the back of a knife. Brush the gâteau with egg glaze and, working from the center, score the top in curves like petals of a flower. NOTE: do not cut through to the filling. Chill 15–20 minutes. Set the oven at 425°F (220°C).

Poke a few holes in the top of the gâteau to allow steam to escape. Bake in preheated oven for 30–35 minutes or until the gâteau is firm, puffed and brown. Sprinkle the top with sugar and broil until shiny. Transfer to a rack to cool.

Croissants
CROISSANTS

There is a legend that attributes the origin of croissants to an Austrian baker who celebrated the victory over the Turks after the seige of Vienna by making pastry in the shape of the Moslem emblem—a crescent.

1–1½ packages dry yeast, or 1–1½ cakes (15–22 g) compressed yeast
1–1¼ cups (2.5–3 dl) lukewarm milk and water, mixed in equal parts
4 cups (500 g) flour
3 tablespoons (40 g) sugar
3 teaspoons (15 g) salt
1 cup (250 g) unsalted butter
1 egg, beaten with ½ teaspoon salt (for glaze)

The amount of yeast necessary depends on how far ahead the dough is made. If making it to bake the same day, use the larger amount. The recipe makes about 32 croissants.

Sprinkle or crumble the yeast over 1 cup (2.5 dl) lukewarm milk and water. Let stand 5 minutes until dissolved. Sift the flour onto a working surface or into a bowl and make a large well in the center. Add the sugar, salt and liquid with the dissolved yeast to the well and mix in the flour quickly and lightly with the fingertips. If the dough is dry, add a little more liquid while mixing. Form a rough ball as for puff pastry; do not knead. Transfer to a greased bowl and cover with a damp cloth. Leave in a warm place ½–1 hour until slightly risen. NOTE: it should puff, but not double in bulk as does normal yeast dough. Deflate the dough by knocking lightly on the top and cover with a damp towel. Chill overnight in the refrigerator.

Six hours later or the next day, flour the butter and lightly pound into a compact square with a rolling pin. Remove the dough from the bowl and roll out to a 15″ (37 cm) square (large enough to wrap around the butter). Set the butter in the center and fold the dough around it like an envelope. Press the seams lightly to seal.

Put the dough seams down on a floured working surface and press with rolling pin 3–4 times to flatten slightly. Roll it out to a rectangle 7–8″ (17–20 cm) wide and 20–24″ (50–60 cm) long. Fold the rectangle in thirds, one end inside with the layers as accurate as possible. If necessary, pull the corners to keep them in a rectangle. Wrap the dough and chill 15 minutes or until firm.

With the open edges towards you and the closed seam to your left side, roll out the dough again to a long rectangle and fold in thirds. Wrap and chill again 15 minutes or until the dough is firm. Repeat this process once more and chill 15 minutes or until firm.

Set the oven to 425° (220°C). *To shape the croissants:* Roll out the dough to a rectangle ⅛″ (3 mm) thick, cut into 4″ (10 cm) squares and cut them in half diagonally. Roll up, starting from the longest side of the triangle. Set the croissants on a buttered baking sheet and leave them straight or curl around the ends, pressing them down well. Cover with a cloth and let rise in a warm place 15–25 minutes or until almost doubled in bulk.

Brush with glaze and bake in preheated oven 5 minutes; turn down the heat to 375°F (190°C) and continue baking about 10 minutes or until browned. Cool on a wire rack.

Croissants are best eaten the day they are baked, but they can be kept 2–3 days in an airtight container, or they can be frozen, baked or unbaked.

GREGORY
USHER

Gregory Usher, the deputy director of La Varenne, has a contagious enthusiasm for food. During demonstrations he can work for just so long before succumbing to temptation and dipping his fingers into whatever is being prepared. Then you'll hear, "Mmmm. Isn't that good? It's what you would choose for a last meal!" And the next day he'll scoop into something else, laugh at himself and repeat, "Oh, there's nothing better! This would be the perfect last meal."

Since a freshman in high school, Gregory has known that cooking was for him. At the University of Oregon, where he majored in art history, he opened a catering business, Entirely Entertaining, on the side. When he switched locales to study at the Sorbonne, he formulated another goal—not only to cook, but to do it in Paris: "Food is loved and appreciated in France. Those who work with it are respected professionals. Meals are events. You need only walk down a street in Paris, any street, to see that the French live, eat and think food."

An American who knows more about French cuisine that most Frenchmen, Gregory frequents the markets and restaurants of his adopted city and each Monday morning regales La Varenne students with reports of the best buy in the markets that week or of the dishes prepared by a newly-discovered young chef.

Before coming to La Varenne in 1976, Gregory gained expertise working under Michel Guérard of nouvelle cuisine and cuisine minceur fame ("He was an inspiration," says Gregory), with Claude Verger at the Barrière Pocquelin and at the fashionable Orangerie restaurant on the Ile St. Louis. At the school he manages both student and administrative affairs; he travels on tour—to Germany, to Venice, to the U.S.A.—and tries to find time to work on a guide to Parisian bistros.

Although he still harbors dreams of opening his own restaurant in Paris—"A combined art gallery and restaurant would be ideal"—he is devoted to the idea of continuing his work at La Varenne: "We are to food what the last two years of Harvard business school are to industry. As well as the mechanics, we teach the art."

GREGORY USHER

Appetizers

Volcano Salad
Camembert Fritters
Cream of Cauliflower Soup
Kipper Mousse

Main Courses

Fillets of Sole with Mushrooms and Tomatoes
Scallops Nantaise
Chicken with Wine Vinegar
Turkey Escalopes with Cream
Veal or Chicken Cutlets
Braised Beef with Olives
Beef Stew with Walnuts
Rabbit with Prunes
Lamb Ragoût

Vegetables

Parisienne Potatoes
Creamed Endives with Ham
Spinach Gratin

Desserts

Oranges with Caramel
Pears in Red Wine with Green Peppercorns
Norwegian Cream
Light Apple Tart

Volcano Salad
SALADE VOLCAN

Salads such as this one that stress unusual combinations of colors and textures are called fantasy salads in France, and are an important element of nouvelle cuisine.

  1 pound (500 g) thin green beans
  Salt and pepper
  3 ounces (90 g) large mushrooms
  Juice of ½ lemon
  2 avocados
  4 tomatoes, peeled, seeded and chopped
  16–20 lettuce leaves
  4 tablespoons corn kernels, cooked

For the Vinaigrette:
  1 tablespoon mustard
  2 tablespoons vinegar
  6 tablespoons (1 dl) oil
  Salt and pepper
  2 shallots, finely chopped

Cook the green beans in a large pan of boiling salted water 5–7 minutes or until barely tender. Drain, refresh under cold running water and drain thoroughly.

For the vinaigrette: Whisk together the mustard and vinegar. Add the oil in a slow stream, whisking constantly to emulsify the dressing, and season to taste. Add the shallots to two-thirds of the vinaigrette, leaving the remaining vinaigrette plain. Mix the shallot vinaigrette with the green beans.

Slice the mushrooms at the last minute, keeping the slices of each together, and sprinkle with lemon juice. Slice the avocados and sprinkle with lemon juice immediately. Season the chopped tomato with salt and pepper and chill.

To serve: On each plate arrange a bed of lettuce. Arrange the green beans in a high dome in the center. Put overlapping avocado slices against one side of the dome and overlapping mushroom slices against the other side. NOTE: together the avocado and mushroom slices form a ring around the beans. Sprinkle the avocado and mushroom slices with the plain vinaigrette. Spoon a little tomato on top of the dome of beans and sprinkle about 1 tablespoon corn kernels over the tomato.

Camembert Fritters

BEIGNETS DE CAMEMBERT

Gregory finds that these fritters are always a big hit at any party because of the intriguing flavor and the contrast of texture between the soft interior and crisp outside. He says, "Take the time to deep fry the parsley and you will really stun your guests."

1 Camembert cheese
3 egg yolks
1 teaspoon Dijon-style mustard
¼ cup (30 g) flour seasoned with ¼ teaspoon each salt
    and pepper
1 egg, beaten to mix with 1 tablespoon water and
    1 tablespoon oil
1 cup (100 g) dry white breadcrumbs
Deep fat (for frying)
Bunch of parsley (for garnish)—optional

For the Thick Béchamel Sauce:
1½ cups (3.75 dl) milk
1 slice of onion
1 bay leaf
6 peppercorns
¼ cup (60 g) butter
6 tablespoons (50 g) flour
Salt and white pepper
Pinch of grated nutmeg

1½" (3.75 cm) plain cookie cutter
These fritters can be cut in 1" (2.5 cm) rounds for delicious cocktail hors d'oeuvre.

Discard the rind and chop the cheese. Make the béchamel sauce (see **Creamed Endives with Ham**), add the cheese and egg yolks and simmer, stirring constantly, 2 minutes or until smooth and very thick. Take from the heat, add the mustard and taste for seasoning. Pour into a buttered tray or cake pan to make a ½" (1.25 cm) layer and chill 2–8 hours in the refrigerator or 30 minutes in the freezer. Warm the tray slightly over heat to melt the butter and cut out 1½" (3.75 cm) rounds of cheese mixture. Coat them with seasoned flour; then brush with beaten egg and coat with breadcrumbs. The fritters can be prepared 24 hours ahead and kept uncovered in the refrigerator, or they can be frozen.

To finish: Heat the deep fat to 360°F (180°C). Fry the fritters, a few at a time, until golden brown and drain thoroughly on paper towels. Keep warm in a 350°F (175°C) oven while frying the rest.

If garnishing with fried parsley, be sure it is dry; let the fat cool slightly, then toss in the parsley; stand back as it will sputter. After 30 seconds, or when sputtering stops, lift out the parsley with a slotted spoon and drain on paper towels. Arrange the fritters overlapping on a platter, sprinkle with fried parsley sprigs and serve at once.

Cream of Cauliflower Soup
CREME DUBARRY

You will be surprised at the delicate flavor of this soup. Serve with either cheese puffs or croûtons.

½ medium cauliflower, divided in flowerets
Salt and pepper
4–5 tablespoons (60–75 g) butter
2 potatoes, thinly sliced
4–5 cups (1–1.25 L) milk or veal stock, or a mixture of both
2 tablespoons chopped chervil or parsley (to finish)

If using Cheese Choux Puffs:
½ cup (75 g) flour
½ cup (1.25 dl) water
¼ teaspoon (1 g) salt
¼ cup (60 g) unsalted butter
2 large eggs
¼ cup (30 g) grated Parmesan cheese

If using Croûtons:
3–4 slices white bread, crusts removed, diced
3–4 tablespoons (45–60 g) oil and butter, mixed

Pastry bag with ⅛" (3 mm) plain tube

The quanity of choux pastry, the smallest it is possible to measure accurately, makes enough puffs for 10–12 people. Leftover puffs can be kept 1–2 days in an airtight container or can be frozen. The soup serves 6.

Blanch the cauliflower in boiling salted water 2 minutes and drain. In a heavy-based pan melt 2 tablespoons (30 g) butter, add the potatoes and press a piece of foil on top. Cover and cook gently, stirring occasionally, 10–15 minutes or until soft. NOTE: do not allow them to brown. Add 4 cups (1 L) milk, stock or a mixture of both, the cauliflower, salt and pepper, cover and simmer 15–20 minutes or until vegetables are very tender. Puree the soup in a blender or food mill. Add more stock or milk if necessary; it should be creamy but not thick. Taste for seasoning. The soup can be made 2 days ahead and kept in the refrigerator, or it can be frozen.

For the cheese puffs: Heat the oven to 400°F (200°C). Make the choux pastry (see **Cheese Puff**) and beat in the grated cheese. Using a pastry bag with a ⅛" (3 mm) plain tube, pipe thimble-sized mounds on a baking sheet. Bake 12–15 minutes or until brown and crisp; cool on a rack. The choux can be made a day or two ahead and kept in an airtight container. They will harden on standing but, as they are added to soup, this does not matter. *Alternatively, make croûtons:* Fry the diced bread in oil and butter until golden brown and drain in a strainer or on paper towels. The croûtons can be made several hours ahead and kept at room temperature.

To finish: Reheat the soup and stir in the chervil or parsley. Take from heat and stir in the remaining butter, piece by piece. Spoon the soup into bowls and serve the puffs or croûtons separately.

Kipper Mousse
MOUSSE DE HARENG FUME

Gregory likes to serve this mousse as an unusual hors d'oeuvre at cocktail parties or buffets. He suggests shaping it as a fish and decorating it accordingly.

> 1 pair (about ¾ pound or 350 g) kipper fillets
> 1¼ cups (3 dl) milk
> ⅓ cup (100 g) unsalted butter
> 2–3 tablespoons heavy cream
> Freshly ground black pepper
> Pinch of cayenne
> Squeeze of lemon juice
> Salt—optional
> Toasted bread (for serving)

Set the oven at 350°F (175°C). Bake the fillets in the milk in a covered dish 12–15 minutes or until they flake easily. Let cool to tepid; then drain and flake the meat, discarding the skin. Push the kipper through a sieve to remove any bones.

Work half the kipper with half the butter and 1 tablespoon cream in a blender, then blend remaining kipper, butter and cream. Alternatively, work them together in an electric food processor, or pound the kipper in a mortar with a pestle and gradually work in the butter and cream.

Season the mousse with pepper, cayenne, lemon juice and salt, if necessary, to taste. NOTE: kippers are often salty and no more salt may be needed. Pile the mousse in a bowl or crock, cover and chill. It can be made up to 48 hours before serving, but it should be left 2–3 hours at room temperature to soften. Serve with hot toast.

Fillets of Sole with Mushrooms and Tomatoes
FILETS DE SOLE D'ANTIN

For this dish Gregory often decorates the platter with fluted mushrooms. Be sure to allow at least one per person. If you like, pipe Duchesse Potatoes around the border of the platter (see **Scallops Nantaise***).*

1½ pounds (750 g) sole fillets
5 tablespoons (75 g) butter
2 shallots, finely chopped
½ pound (250 g) mushrooms, thinly sliced
2 tomatoes, peeled, seeded and coarsely chopped
Salt and white pepper
½ cup (1.25 dl) fish stock (see **Stuffed Sole with Whiskey Sauce**)
½ cup (1.25 dl) white wine
3 tablespoons (20 g) flour
¼ cup (6 cl) heavy cream
3 egg yolks
6 tablespoons (1 dl) water
1 tablespoon chopped parsley

The recipe serves 8 as an appetizer or 4 as a main course.

Wash and dry the sole fillets. Flatten by placing them between two pieces of moistened waxed paper and pounding with the flat part of a heavy knife. Butter a sauté pan or shallow casserole with 1 tablespoon (15 g) butter, sprinkle with the shallots and add the mushrooms, tomatoes, salt and pepper. Fold the sole fillets in half, skin side inwards, and set them tail end underneath on the vegetables. Pour the fish stock and wine over the fish, cover with buttered foil and simmer gently 7–10 minutes or until the fish is just tender. Let cool slightly, then lift out the fillets and drain on paper towels. Transfer to a platter and keep warm.

To finish: Boil the cooking liquid with the vegetables until reduced to about 1½ cups (3.75 dl). With a fork mash 3 tablespoons (45 g) butter with the flour until smooth. Whisk in the butter-flour mixture piece by piece, adding enough to thicken the sauce slightly. Simmer for 2 minutes, then add cream. In a separate small saucepan cook the egg yolks and water over low heat, whisking vigorously, until very frothy and slightly thickened. NOTE: they will curdle if overcooked. Whisk the yolks into the sauce. NOTE: the sauce cannot be reheated after the yolks are added. Add the remaining tablespoon (15 g) butter in small pieces, shaking until incorporated; then add parsley. Taste for seasoning, spoon over the fish and brown under the broiler.

This dish cannot be prepared ahead and reheated. However, the cooked fish can be covered and kept warm in a low oven up to 15 minutes. The sauce can be kept hot in a water bath, then spooned over the fish and browned just before serving.

Scallops Nantaise
COQUILLES ST. JACQUES NANTAISE

Be careful with the curry powder and cayenne so they don't overpower the delicate flavor of the scallops.

6 tablespoons (90 g) butter
1 large onion, finely chopped
1½ pounds (750 g) sea or bay scallops
¼ cup (30 g) flour seasoned with ¼ teaspoon salt and
    pinch of pepper
½ teaspoon curry powder, or to taste
Pinch of cayenne
2 tablespoons brandy
½ cup (1.25 dl) white wine
3 tomatoes, peeled, seeded and coarsely chopped, or 2 cups or
    1 pound (5 dl or 500 g) canned tomatoes, drained
    and chopped
Salt and freshly ground black pepper—optional
3 tablespoons browned breadcrumbs

For the Duchesse Potatoes:
3–4 medium potatoes (1½ pounds or 750 g), peeled and halved
Salt and white pepper
3 tablespoons (45 g) butter
Pinch of grated nutmeg
3 egg yolks

4 deep scallop shells
Pastry bag with medium star tube

For the duchesse potatoes: Put the potatoes in a pan of cold salted water, cover and bring to a boil. Simmer 15–20 minutes or until tender. Drain, return to the pan and dry, stirring, over very low heat 5 minutes. While still hot, work them through a sieve or ricer and return them to the pan. Beat in the butter with salt, pepper and nutmeg and continue beating over heat until light and fluffy. Take from heat and beat in the egg yolks. Keep covered until ready to use.

In a sauté pan or skillet, melt half the butter and cook the onion slowly until soft but not brown. Cut sea scallops in 2–3 rounds but leave bay scallops whole; toss in seasoned flour to coat lightly. Add the scallops to the pan and sauté over brisk heat, stirring occasionally, 3–4 minutes or until golden brown. Halfway through cooking, sprinkle with curry powder and cayenne.

When the scallops are brown, add the brandy and flame. Add the wine and tomatoes and simmer 3–5 minutes until the wine is well reduced and the tomatoes pulpy. NOTE: do not overcook the scallops or they will toughen. If there is too much liquid, remove the scallops and boil to reduce. Taste for seasoning and return the scallops to the liquid. Spoon the mixture into the shells. Using a piping bag with a medium star tube, pipe a border of potato around the shells. Melt the remaining butter. Sprinkle the scallops with browned breadcrumbs, then with melted butter. The scallops can be prepared 24 hours ahead and kept in the refrigerator, or they can be frozen.

Just before serving, set the oven at 425°F (220°C) or heat the broiler. Bake the scallops 10–12 minutes or heat under the broiler until very hot and browned.

Chicken with Wine Vinegar
POULET AU VINAIGRE DE VIN

Though the amount of garlic in this recipe seems huge, you will discover that the garlic flavor is really quite mild in the end.

> 3 pound (1.5 kg) roasting chicken, cut in 8 pieces
> Salt and pepper
> 6 tablespoons (90 g) butter
> 15 cloves garlic, unpeeled
> 1¼ cups (3 dl) wine vinegar
> 2 ripe tomatoes, coarsely chopped
> 1 tablespoon tomato paste
> Bouquet garni
> 1 cup (2.5 dl) chicken stock
> Chervil sprigs (for decoration)

Season the pieces of chicken with salt and pepper. In a sauté pan, heat 1 tablespoon (15 g) butter and add the pieces of chicken, skin side down, starting with the legs and thighs because they need the longest cooking. When they begin to brown, add the wing pieces and finally the breast pieces; when all are brown, turn them over and brown the other side for 1–2 minutes.

Add the garlic, cover and cook over low heat 20 minutes. Holding the cover to prevent the pieces of chicken from falling out, pour off the excess fat. Add the vinegar and simmer about 10 minutes until well reduced. Add the tomatoes, tomato paste and bouquet garni and simmer 10 more minutes. Transfer the chicken to a platter and keep warm. Add the stock and boil until very well reduced and concentrated in flavor. Taste for seasoning and strain, pressing hard on the garlic.

To finish: Reheat the sauce, remove from the heat and whisk in the remaining butter in small pieces, a few at a time. Taste for seasoning, pour over the chicken and decorate with a few sprigs of chervil.

Turkey Escalopes with Cream
ESCALOPES DE DINDE A LA CREME

These escalopes blend with many accompaniments. Gregory suggests, "I often opt for fresh green noodles as the color is so attractive."

1½ pounds (750 g) turkey breasts
½ cup (75 g) flour seasoned with ½ teaspoon salt and
    ¼ teaspoon pepper
4–5 tablespoons (60–75 g) butter
¾ cup (2 dl) white wine
¾ cup (2 dl) white chicken or veal stock
½ pound (250 g) mushrooms, thinly sliced
½ cup (1.25 dl) heavy cream
Salt and pepper
1 tablespoon chopped parsley (for sprinkling)

Cut the turkey breasts in thin slices (escalopes) and flatten them to ¼" (6 mm) by beating between pieces of waxed paper with a rolling pin. Coat them with seasoned flour, patting to remove the excess. In a sauté pan, melt 3 tablespoons (45 g) butter and sauté several escalopes over medium heat until browned, allowing 2–3 minutes on each side. Arrange them overlapping on a platter and keep warm. Sauté the remaining escalopes in the same way, adding more butter if necessary.

Deglaze the pan with the wine and stock, add the mushrooms and simmer until the sauce is slightly thick. Add the cream, bring just to a boil, taste for seasoning and spoon over the escalopes.

The escalopes can be cooked up to 48 hours ahead and kept in the sauce in the refrigerator. They can also be frozen. Reheat over medium heat, taking care not to overcook them. Sprinkle with parsley and serve.

Veal or Chicken Cutlets
POJARSKI

Because this Pojarski mixture has no starch or egg to bind the ground meat, handle with care, especially when turning the cutlets.

1½ pounds (750 g) lean veal or boned chicken breast
Salt and pepper
1½ cups (3.75 dl) heavy cream
Flour (for shaping)
¼ pound (125 g) mushrooms, thinly sliced
Squeeze of lemon juice
3 tablespoons (45 g) butter
3 tablespoons brandy
½ cup (1.25 dl) wine
1 tablespoon chopped parsley (for sprinkling)

For the cutlets: Work the veal or chicken through the fine plate of a grinder once or twice until very finely ground. Beat it with a wooden spoon or with the dough hook of an electric mixer 3–4 minutes or until it leaves the sides of the bowl in a ball. Alternatively, work the meat in an electric food processor. NOTE: this beating gives the Pojarski a light smooth texture. Add plenty of salt and pepper and beat in half the cream, 1 tablespoon at a time, beating well after each addition. If using an electric food processor, add the cream in a steady stream and stop beating as soon as it is mixed. NOTE: if overworked, it tends to liquify. Divide the meat into 4–6 parts and, on a lightly floured board, mold each into a cutlet shape about 1" (2.5 cm) thick.

Put the mushrooms in a buttered pan with the lemon juice, 2 tablespoons water, salt and pepper and cover with buttered paper and lid. Cook gently 3–4 minutes until tender. The mushrooms and cutlets can be prepared up to 6 hours ahead; keep them covered in the refrigerator.

To finish: In a skillet melt the butter and sauté the cutlets over medium heat 4–5 minutes on each side or until lightly browned. Add the brandy and flame. Arrange the cutlets, overlapping, on a platter and keep warm. Add the wine to the pan, simmer until well reduced and add the mushrooms and their liquid with the remaining cream. Bring just to a boil and taste for seasoning. Spoon over the cutlets, sprinkle with chopped parsley and serve.

Braised Beef with Olives
DAUBE ORLEANAISE

Gregory is very fond of dishes that simmer gently for hours, like this daube. In contrast to the marinade in **Rabbit with Prunes***, here the marinade is cooked before being poured over the beef so its flavor will be more concentrated.*

> 4 pounds (2 kg) round or chuck roast of beef
> ½ pound (250 g) salt pork, diced
> ⅓ cup (1 dl) rum
> 1 pound (500 g) tomatoes, peeled, seeded and chopped
> 2 cloves garlic, crushed
> 2 tablespoons chopped fresh basil, or 1 teaspoon dried basil
> Salt and freshly ground black pepper
> 1 cup (150 g) pimiento-stuffed olives
> 1 tablespoon chopped fresh basil or parsley (for sprinkling)
>
> **For the Marinade:**
> 2 tablespoons olive oil
> 1 tablespoon wine vinegar
> 2 cups (5 dl) red wine
> 1 large onion, chopped
> 1 large carrot, chopped
> 1 large bouquet garni
> Strip of lemon rind
> 6 peppercorns
>
> The daube serves 6.

Bring all the ingredients for the marinade to a boil in a saucepan (not aluminum). Cool completely. Put the beef in a deep bowl and pour the marinade over the beef. Cover and refrigerate for 3 days, turning the beef several times.

Set the oven to 300°F (150°C). Strain and reserve both the marinade and the vegetables. Blanch the salt pork by putting in cold water, bringing to a boil and simmering 5 minutes. Drain. In a deep casserole, brown the salt pork and remove it. Brown the beef on all sides over medium heat, remove it and discard all but 1 tablespoon of fat from the pan. Pat the reserved vegetables dry, add to the pan and cook 5–7 minutes over low heat until slightly soft. Return the beef to the pan, add the rum and flame.

Add the salt pork, tomatoes, garlic, basil, salt, pepper and strained marinade. Cover, bring to a boil and braise in heated oven 3–4 hours or until meat is tender enough to cut with a spoon. The daube can be prepared up to 3 days ahead and kept in the refrigerator, or it can be frozen.

To finish: If necessary reheat the daube in a 350°F (175°C) oven for an hour or until very hot. Transfer to a carving board and keep warm. Skim any fat from the sauce, add the olives, taste for seasoning and bring just back to a boil. Carve a few slices of the meat and arrange overlapping on a platter with the remaining meat at the end. Spoon over a little sauce and sprinkle with basil or parsley. Serve the remaining sauce separately.

Beef Stew with Walnuts
RAGOUT DE BOEUF AUX NOIX

Be sure to brown the pieces of beef on all sides over high heat, or their juices will escape and the meat will stew instead of browning.

4 tablespoons oil
1½–2 pounds (750 g–1 kg) beef chuck, cut in 2″ (5 cm) cubes
2 onions, sliced
1 carrot, sliced
1 stalk celery, sliced
2 cloves garlic, crushed
3 tablespoons (20 g) flour
1 cup (2.5 dl) red wine
2 cups (5 dl) brown veal or beef stock
Bouquet garni
Salt and freshly ground black pepper

For the Garnish:
½ bunch of celery, cut in ½″ (1.25 cm) slices
2 tablespoons (30 g) butter
Salt
¾ cup (100 g) walnut halves
Pared rind of 1 orange, cut in needle-like strips

In a heavy-based casserole, heat the oil and brown the beef cubes, a few at a time. Remove them and add the onions, carrot and celery. Cook slowly, stirring occasionally, until soft but not brown. Add the garlic and cook 1–2 more minutes. Add the flour and cook, stirring, until a rich brown. NOTE: do not allow it to burn. Add wine, stock, bouquet garni, salt and pepper. Return the meat to the pan and bring the stew to a boil. Cover tightly and simmer on top of the stove or in a 350°F (175°C) oven 2–2½ hours or until very tender. If the sauce is not thick, remove the lid during the last half hour of cooking so it reduces. Transfer the beef to another pan and strain the sauce over it. The meat can be cooked up to 3 days ahead. Cool and keep covered in the refrigerator or freeze.

A short time before serving, prepare the garnish: Cook the celery slowly in the butter, stirring occasionally, 5–7 minutes or until soft but not brown. Sprinkle with salt, add the walnuts, mix well and take from the heat. Put the orange rind in cold water, bring to a boil, boil 3–4 minutes, refresh under cold running water and drain thoroughly. Reheat the stew if necessary, taste for seasoning and spoon into a serving dish. Reheat the celery and walnut mixture if necessary and sprinkle it and the orange rind over the stew. Serve immediately.

Rabbit with Prunes
LAPIN AUX PRUNEAUX

Marinating adds flavor and moistness to the rabbit. Prunes are used as a garnish in several French country dishes, especially with rabbit and pork.

> 1 rabbit, cut in 5–6 pieces
> ½ pound (250 g) prunes
> 1 tablespoon oil
> 1 tablespoon (15 g) butter
> 2 tablespoons (15 g) flour
> 1 cup (2.5 dl) red wine
> 1 cup (2.5 dl) veal or chicken stock
> 1 clove garlic, crushed
> Bouquet garni
> Salt and freshly ground black pepper
> 1 tablespoon chopped parsley (for sprinkling)

> **For the Marinade:**
> ½ cup (1.25 dl) red wine
> Large bouquet garni
> 1 onion, coarsely chopped
> 1 carrot, coarsely chopped
> 6 peppercorns, slightly crushed
> 1 tablespoon oil

Combine marinade ingredients and marinate rabbit at room temperature, turning occasionally, for 4–12 hours or in the refrigerator for 1–2 days. Pour boiling water or tea over the prunes, cover and leave to soak about 3 hours.

Drain the rabbit and pat dry. In a sauté pan or shallow casserole heat the oil and butter and brown the rabbit pieces on all sides. Remove from pan, add the onion and carrot from the marinade and sauté lightly until they soften. Sprinkle the flour over the vegetables and cook, stirring, until well browned. Add the marinade and wine and bring to a boil. Add the stock, garlic, bouquet garni and seasoning. Replace the rabbit pieces. Drain the prunes, add to the pan, cover and simmer 35–45 minutes or until the rabbit is tender. It can be cooked up to 3 days ahead and kept covered in the refrigerator, or it can be frozen.

To serve: Reheat the rabbit if it has been cooked ahead, transfer it to a serving dish and spoon over the prunes. Strain the sauce. Reduce if necessary to a thin coating consistency, taste for seasoning and spoon over the rabbit. Sprinkle with parsley just before serving.

Lamb Ragoût
RAGOUT D'AGNEAU

This lamb stew is made with as many fresh vegetables as possible; in winter they may be reduced to potatoes, carrots and onions, and the meat is mutton. In spring, it is made with baby lamb and new vegetables.

1½ pounds (750 g) boned shoulder or breast of lamb,
    cut in 1½" (3.75 cm) pieces
Salt and freshly ground black pepper
2 tablespoons oil
2 tablespoons (15 g) flour
1 tablespoon tomato paste
1 clove garlic, crushed
Bouquet garni
2–2½ cups (5–6.25 dl) stock
1 teaspoon arrowroot, mixed to a paste with 1 tablespoon
    water—optional

For the Garnish:
12–16 baby onions
2 tomatoes, peeled, seeded and chopped
8 baby carrots, peeled, or 2 large carrots, quartered
1 turnip, cut in 8 pieces
1½ pounds (750 g) small new potatoes, peeled, or 3–4 large
    potatoes, quartered
1 cup (150 g) shelled fresh peas, or half a 10-ounce (300 g)
    package frozen peas
2 tablespoons chopped parsley

Set the oven at 425°F (220°C). Season the meat with salt and pepper. In a casserole, heat the oil and brown the lamb on all sides, a few pieces at a time. Take them out, add the onions from the garnish and brown them also. Remove them, replace the meat and sprinkle with flour. Cook 5 minutes in the preheated oven or until the flour is browned. Remove the casserole from the oven, let cool slightly and add tomato paste, garlic, bouquet garni and enough stock to cover the meat. Cover and simmer 1 hour. Transfer the meat to another casserole, skim any fat from the sauce and strain it over the meat. If necessary, thicken it to a light coating consistency by stirring the arrowroot paste into the boiling liquid and heating gently.

For the garnish: Add the tomatoes and carrots with more stock to cover if necessary, cover the pan and continue simmering 30 minutes. Add the turnip, potatoes and onions and simmer 10 minutes longer. Meanwhile, blanch the fresh peas in boiling water for 2 minutes, refresh and drain thoroughly. Add them to the meat and continue cooking 20 minutes or until the lamb is tender. If using frozen peas, add them 8–10 minutes before the end of cooking. Taste for seasoning, sprinkle with parsley and serve the ragoût very hot.

Parisienne Potatoes
POMMES DE TERRE PARISIENNE

The French have managed to do marvelous things with potatoes, once they realized in the 18th century that potatoes were not poisonous. Parisienne potatoes are an important garnish in many classic French meat dishes.

> 5–6 large .potatoes (about 2 pounds or 1 kg), peeled
> 1 tablespoon oil
> 3 tablespoons (45 g) butter
> Salt and pepper
>
> *¾–1" (2–2.5 cm) ball cutter*

Use the cutter to cut the potatoes in balls. To make the frying easier and quicker, you may blanch them: cover with cold water, bring to a boil, drain and dry well.

In a skillet or frying pan heat the oil and butter, add the potato balls and sauté 10–15 minutes until tender, shaking the pan from time to time so they brown evenly. Start over high heat to sear the outside, then lower the heat to cook them through. Sprinkle with salt and pepper just before serving. The potatoes can be cooked 15–20 minutes ahead and kept warm in a low oven.

Creamed Endives with Ham
ENDIVES AU JAMBON A LA CREME

Says Gregory, "This was one of my first impressions of France and to me it remains typical—a standard favorite in many French households."

8–10 heads (about 2 pounds or 1 kg) Belgian endive
3 tablespoons (45 g) butter
1 teaspoon sugar
Salt and pepper
8–10 slices cooked ham
½ cup (60 g) grated Gruyère or Parmesan cheese (for sprinkling)

For the Béchamel Sauce:
3 cups (7.5 dl) milk
1 slice of onion
1 bay leaf
8 peppercorns
¼ cup (60 g) butter
5½ tablespoons (45 g) flour
Salt and white pepper
Pinch of grated nutmeg

The recipe serves 8 as an appetizer or vegetable, or 4 as a main dish.

Set the oven at 350°F (175°C). Wipe the endives, discard any wilted leaves and trim the stems. With the point of a knife, hollow the stems so the endives cook more evenly. Spread the butter in a casserole, put in the endives and sprinkle with sugar, salt and pepper. Cover and bake 1 hour or until very tender.

For the béchamel sauce: Scald the milk. Add the onion, bay leaf and peppercorns and let infuse 5–10 minutes. In a heavy-based saucepan melt the butter, whisk in the flour and cook 1–2 minutes until foaming but not browned; let cool. Strain in the hot milk, whisk well; then bring to a boil, whisking constantly. Simmer 2–3 minutes and season to taste with salt, pepper and nutmeg.

Let the endives cool slightly; then roll each in a slice of ham and arrange diagonally in a buttered, shallow baking dish. Spoon the sauce on top and sprinkle with the cheese. The endives can be prepared 24 hours ahead and kept covered in the refrigerator.

To finish: Set the oven at 400°F (200°C). Bake the endives 20–25 minutes or until very hot and browned.

Spinach Gratin
GRATIN D'EPINARDS

"Nothing is better than fresh spinach," says Gregory, and this gratin recipe is an elegant accompaniment for chops or broiled fish.

1½ pounds (750 g) fresh spinach, or two 10-ounce (300 g) packages frozen spinach
Salt and pepper
5 tablespoons (75 g) butter
2 tablepoons heavy cream
Pinch of grated nutmeg
1 cup (2.5 dl) light cream
2 tablespoons (15 g) flour
½ cup (60 g) grated Gruyère cheese

Discard the stems from fresh spinach and wash the leaves in several changes of water. Cook in plenty of boiling salted water, stirring occasionally, 5 minutes or until the leaves are wilted. Drain, refresh with cold water and drain thoroughly. Squeeze by handfuls to extract all the water. Thaw frozen spinach and squeeze out excess liquid. Chop the spinach. Heat 2 tablespoons (30 g) of the butter, add the spinach and stir over the heat for a minute to dry it. Add the heavy cream and continue stirring another minute. Season with salt, pepper and nutmeg.

Scald the light cream. In a heavy-based pan, melt 2 tablespoons (30 g) more butter, whisk in the flour and cook 1–2 minutes until foaming but not browned. Let cool, then add the hot cream, whisking. Bring to a boil, whisking constantly, and simmer 2–3 minutes. Take from the heat, let cool several minutes and add half the cheese with salt and pepper to taste. Spoon a little sauce on the bottom of a lightly buttered, shallow ovenproof dish. Pile the spinach on top. Coat with the remaining sauce, sprinkle with the remaining cheese and dribble on the rest of the butter, melted. The dish can be assembled up to 2 days ahead and kept covered in the refrigerator, or it can be frozen.

To finish: Reheat the spinach if necessary in a 350°F (175°C) oven. Brown under a hot broiler and serve.

Oranges with Caramel

ORANGES AU CARAMEL

Gregory often uses a food processor to chop the hardened caramel. Sometimes he sprinkles only a little of it over the oranges and passes the rest in a small glass bowl so guests can help themselves.

8 large seedless oranges
1 tablespoon Grand Marnier

For the Poaching Syrup:
½ cup (100 g) sugar
2 cups (5 dl) water
1 tablespoon Grand Marnier

For the Caramel:
1½ cups (300 g) sugar
1 cup (2.5 dl) cold water
½ cup (1.25 dl) warm water

Pare the orange rind from the oranges and cut it in needle-like shreds with a sharp knife. Blanch the rind in boiling water 3–4 minutes, refresh with cold water and drain. Make poaching syrup by bringing to a boil the sugar, water and Grand Marnier. Add the blanched rinds and poach 10–15 minutes or until the rinds are tender and the syrup is thick.

With a serrated or very sharp knife, cut the pith and outer skin from all the oranges, using a sawing motion and cutting in a spiral. NOTE: hold the oranges over a bowl while peeling to catch any juice and add it to the simmering orange rinds. Cut the oranges crosswise in ³/₈" (1 cm) slices, reshape and spear with a toothpick to hold together. Pile in a bowl.

For the caramel: Oil a baking sheet. Heat the sugar and 1 cup (2.5 dl) water until dissolved, then boil steadily without stirring to a deep golden caramel. Remove from heat and, when the bubbles have subsided, pour half the caramel onto the prepared baking sheet. Add the warm water to the remaining caramel in the pan; stand back as it will sputter. Bring back to a boil, stirring to dissolve the caramel, and add the orange rinds with their syrup. Let cool; then put a heaping tablespoon of orange rind on each orange, carefully pour on the sauce, sprinkle with 1 tablespoon Grand Marnier and chill. When the caramel on the baking sheet is cold and hard, crush it with a rolling pin or in a mortar with pestle; keep in an airtight container. Keep the caramel and oranges covered in the refrigerator.

Just before serving, sprinkle the oranges with crushed caramel. NOTE: the crisp caramel quickly dissolves in contact with moisture, so it must be added at the last minute.

Pears in Red Wine with Green Peppercorns
POIRES AU VIN ROUGE AU POIVRE VERT

Be sure to let poached fruit cool in the syrup, even though this takes longer, so it will absorb as much flavor as possible from the syrup. The dessert is especially attractive served from a shallow glass bowl.

8 firm pears
½ cup (100 g) sugar
2–2½ cups (5–6.25 dl) red wine
Strip of lemon peel
2" (5 cm) piece cinnamon stick
1 teaspoon green peppercorns, drained
Few drops lemon juice—optional

For the Chantilly Cream: (for serving)—optional
¾ cup (2 dl) heavy cream
2 teaspoons sugar
½ teaspoon vanilla extract

Choose a saucepan in which the pears just fit when standing upright. In it heat the sugar, red wine, lemon peel, cinnamon stick and green peppercorns until the sugar is dissolved; then boil 5 minutes and let cool slightly. Peel the pears and core them carefully from the base but leave the stalk. Cut a thin slice off the bottom so they stand up. Immerse them in the syrup, adding more wine if necessary to cover. Cover with the lid and poach 20–45 minutes or until tender. NOTE: cooking time depends on the variety and ripeness of the pears, but 20 minutes is a minimum to prevent discoloration around the cores.

Let the pears cool to tepid in the syrup, then drain them and arrange in a shallow dish. Strain the syrup and reduce until thick (do not allow it to caramelize); taste and add sugar or lemon juice if necessary. Let cool slightly, spoon over pears and chill thoroughly. The pears can be cooked 24 hours ahead and kept tightly covered in the refrigerator.

For the Chantilly cream: In a chilled bowl whip the cream until it starts to thicken. Add the sugar and vanilla and continue beating until the cream holds a shape and sticks to the whisk. Serve the cream separately.

Norwegian Cream
CREME NORVEGIENNE

As the custard for this cream bakes, check to see that the water bath does not boil; if the water boils, the finished custard will not be smooth.

3 tablespoons apricot jam
1 egg white
2 tablespoons (30 g) sugar
½ cup (1.25 dl) heavy cream, whipped until it holds a
   soft shape
½ teaspoon vanilla extract
2 ounces (60 g) semi-sweet chocolate, grated (for sprinkling)

For the Custard:
2 cups (5 dl) milk
3 tablespoons (45 g) sugar
1 vanilla bean, or ½ teaspoon vanilla extract
2 eggs
3 egg yolks

4 ramekins (1 cup or 2.5 dl capacity), or
   1 soufflé dish (1 quart or 1 L capacity)

Set the oven at 350°F (175°C). Melt the jam, spread in the bottom of the dishes and cool.

For the custard: Heat the milk with the sugar until dissolved. Add the vanilla bean, cover and leave to infuse over low heat for 10–15 minutes. Beat the eggs and yolks until frothy and stir in the milk. If using vanilla extract, add it now. Leave to cool. Strain into the prepared dishes, cover with foil and tie with string.

Set the dishes in a water bath, bring just to a boil on top of the stove and bake 20–25 minutes for ramekins or 30–40 minutes for a soufflé dish, or until a knife inserted in the center of the custard comes out clean. Let cool; then chill. The custard can be cooked 48 hours ahead and kept, tightly covered, in the refrigerator.

Not more than 3 hours before serving, whip the egg white until stiff, add the sugar and continue beating until glossy. Fold it into the whipped cream with the vanilla. Sprinkle the custard with half the grated chocolate, cover it completely with the whipped topping and sprinkle with the remaining chocolate.

Light Apple Tart
TARTE AUX POMMES LEGERE

This modern version of a traditional favorite should be almost as thin as a crêpe. The oven should be as hot as possible so the pastry and apples cook and the sugar caramelizes, all at the same time.

8 Golden Delicious apples, peeled, halved and cored
⅓ cup (100 g) butter, cold
½ cup (100 g) granulated sugar

For the Pie Pastry Dough:
2⅓ cups (300 g) flour
¾ cup (200 g) unsalted butter
2 teaspoons (10 g) salt
5–7 tablespoons cold water

Two 10" (25 cm) pie or tart pans

The recipe makes two tarts.

For the pie pastry: Sift the flour onto a working surface and make a large well in the center. Pound the butter to soften it slightly. Put butter, salt and 5 tablespoons water in the well and work together with the fingertips until partly mixed. Gradually work in the flour, pulling the dough into large crumbs. If the crumbs are dry, add up to 2 tablespoons more water, a little at a time. Using a dough scraper, cut the dough to mix. When the dough is nearly smooth, work it lightly on the working surface by pushing it away with the heel of the hand and gathering it up with the dough scraper until it is pliable. NOTE: because of the high proportion of butter, you must be especially careful not to overwork this dough. Press the dough into a ball, wrap and chill at least 30 minutes.

Heat the oven to 475°F (250°C). Roll out the dough to two very thin rounds (about 1/16" or 1.5 mm thick) and line the bases, not sides, of the pans. Unlike most pie pastry, the dough should be stretched, instead of being slid gently into the pan. Prick the dough with a fork.

Cut the apples in very thin slices and arrange one layer of slices on the dough, rounded sides out, in concentric circles. NOTE: to prevent burning, overlap the apple slices slightly so the dough is completely covered with apples. Cut the butter in thin strips. Sprinkle the apples with sugar and arrange the strips of butter on top at approximately equal intervals. Bake in the preheated oven 10–15 minutes or until the apples are tender and the sugar is caramelized. Serve hot. The tarts can be baked ahead and reheated in a hot oven.

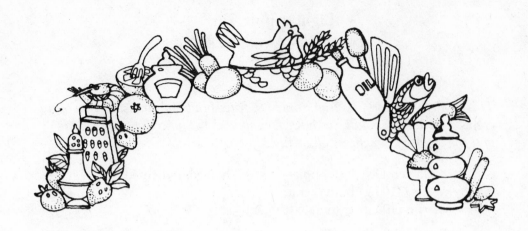

CLAUDE
VAUGUET

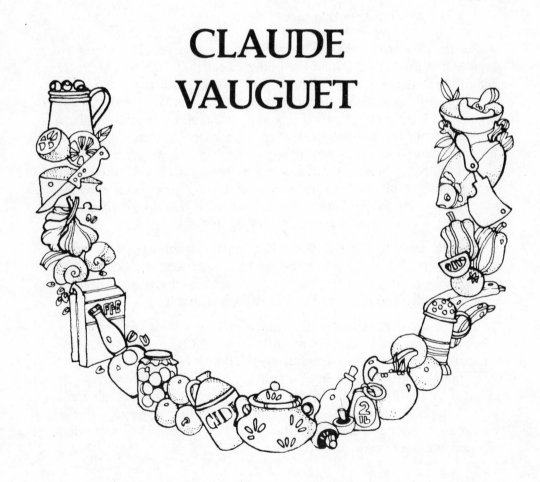

The popular image of a French chef as a temperamental artist is belied by Claude Vauguet—a man of imperturbable humor. Under his tutelage La Varenne students painstakingly reduce onions, carrots and mounds of mushrooms to the required fine, uniform dice. The chef chops with mechanical speed and regularity, the blade unwavering as he casually looks up to make a comment or a joke. He may tease Americans about being too gadget-minded in the kitchen (dark-eyed Chef Vauguet is French to the core), then turn from chopping to the next task, pick up a native implement, grin and say, "In France it's not a gadget but a little appliance." Claude's special province is meats which, in true Gallic fashion, he tests with a pinch. The thumb and forefinger tell him whether a ragoût is almost done or perfectly tender; a poke lets him know whether a fillet of beef is medium or medium rare.

Such abilities must be developed. Chef Vauguet began his apprenticeship at fourteen, working twelve-hour days at a restaurant in the Loire, a region famous for fruits, delicious fish and its delicate *sauce beurre blanc.* At seventeen he came to Paris to work under the illustrious and demanding two-star chef Fernand Chambrette. In addition to moving up through the ranks to become Chef Chambrette's top assistant, Claude has catered parties, cooked for an officer's mess in Algeria during his military service and worked as a maître d'hôtel. He's also bringing up two sons, the elder of whom is now in his teens and starting his own apprenticeship with a top Paris *pâtissier.*

Claude has been with La Varenne since 1977 and says, "I work harder here than I would in a restaurant because so many dishes are in our repertoire, but part of the fun is that no day of the year is the same. Who's ever heard of a restaurant with one thousand five hundred recipes?"

CLAUDE VAUGUET

Appetizers
Morel Boats
Cheese Puff
Scrambled Eggs Magda
Ham Cornets
Terrine of Duck with Orange

Main Courses
Sea Bass Fillets with Vegetable Julienne
Provençal Scallops
Bouillabaisse
Shellfish Quiche
Turban of Sole
Chicken Breasts with Port
Stuffed Veal Breast
Beef Stroganoff
Pork Chops Dijonnaise
Crown Roast of Lamb

Vegetables
Cucumber Gratin
Stuffed Eggplant Imam Bayeldi
Tourte of Green Vegetables
Spinach Mold
Braised Celery

Desserts
Souffléd Oranges
Snow Eggs
Caramel-Glazed Puffs
Normandy Pear Pie

Morel Boats

BARQUETTES AUX MORILLES

In spite of his traditional background, Chef Claude is not against using machines. He often makes the pastry dough for this recipe in an electric food processor.

½ pound (250 g) fresh morels, or 4 ounces (125 g) dried morels
3 tablespoons (45 g) butter
1 onion, finely chopped
Salt and freshly ground black pepper
Pinch of grated nutmeg
2 tablespoons (15 g) flour
1¼ cups (3 dl) heavy cream
Pie pastry (see **Normandy Pear Pie**)
1 tablespoon chopped parsley (for garnish)

2½" (6 cm) boat molds

The morels can also be served (without the pastry boats) as an accompaniment. The recipe makes about 20 boats.

Soak dried morels 3–4 hours in cold water to cover; drain and chop. Wash fresh morels in several changes of water, brushing to remove all the sand, and chop. In a sauté pan melt the butter and cook the onions slowly until soft but not brown. Add the morels with salt, pepper and nutmeg and cook briskly, stirring, 4–5 minutes until tender. NOTE: if cooked too slowly they will be watery. Stir in the flour, cook 1 minute, then add the cream. Bring to a boil, stirring, taste for seasoning and simmer 5–6 minutes. The morels can be prepared up to 2 days ahead and kept covered in the refrigerator.

Make the pastry dough and chill 30 minutes. Set the oven at 400°F (200°C). Roll out the dough to just under ¼" (6 mm) thick. Arrange molds close together near the dough. Roll dough loosely onto the rolling pin and then unroll it over the molds. Take a small piece of dough, dip it in flour and use it to work the dough down into each boat. Roll the rolling pin over the tops of the molds to cut the pastry. Prick the bases, line the molds with pieces of waxed paper and fill with dried beans. Alternatively, put a smaller buttered boat mold inside each. Bake about 8 minutes or until lightly browned. Remove paper and beans or smaller molds, then continue baking the shells 3–4 minutes. They may be made ahead and stored in an airtight container for 3–4 days.

Just before serving: Heat the boats in a low oven. Reheat the morels and spoon into the heated shells. Sprinkle with parsley and serve immediately.

Cheese Puff
GOUGERE

Gougère was originally plain choux pastry flavored with cheese. Here a richer option includes a filling.

For the Cheese Choux Pastry:
⅔ cup (110 g) flour
⅔ cup (1.8 dl) water
¼ teaspoon (1 g) salt
⅓ cup (75 g) butter
3–4 eggs
½ cup (60 g) diced Gruyère cheese
Pinch of pepper

For the Béchamel Filling—optional:
2 cups (5 dl) milk
1 slice of onion
1 bay leaf
6 peppercorns
2½ tablespoons (40 g) butter
¼ cup (30 g) flour
Salt and pepper
Pinch of grated nutmeg
One of the following:
   1 cup (150 g) cooked ham, diced
   1 cup (150 g) cooked chicken, diced
   ⅓ pound (150 g) mushrooms, quartered and sautéed in
     1 tablespoon (15 g) butter
   ½ cup (60 g) grated Gruyère cheese and 2 tablespoons
     heavy cream

8–9" (20–23 cm) pie pan, or ovenproof baking dish

Set the oven at 400°F (200°C). *For the cheese choux pastry:* Sift the flour. In a saucepan heat the water, salt and butter until the butter is melted, then bring just to a boil and take from the heat. Immediately add all the flour and beat vigorously with a wooden spoon for a few seconds until the mixture is smooth and pulls away from the sides of the pan. Beat ½–1 minute over low heat to dry the mixture. Set aside one egg and beat it. Beat the remaining eggs into the dough, one by one. Beat in enough of reserved egg to make a mixture that is very shiny and just falls from the spoon. Stir in the diced cheese and add pepper to taste.

Butter the pie pan or baking dish well and drop the dough by table-spoonfuls around the edge, leaving a hollow in the center. Bake in preheated oven 30–40 minutes or until puffed and brown. The gougère may be served hot, warm or at room temperature.

If adding the filling: Scald the milk. Add the onion, bay leaf and pep-percorns and let infuse 5–10 minutes to add flavor. In a heavy-based sauce-pan melt the butter, whisk in the flour and cook 1–2 minutes until foaming but not browned; let cool. Strain in the hot milk, whisk well, then bring the sauce to a boil, whisking constantly. Reduce to a simmer, add salt, pep-per and nutmeg to taste and continue cooking 3–5 minutes. Add any of the flavorings listed. Rub with butter to prevent the formation of a skin.

When the gougère is baked, spoon the filling into the center and return to the oven 3–5 minutes to reheat. Serve at once.

Scrambled Eggs Magda

OEUFS BROUILLES MAGDA

The French take scrambled eggs seriously, and Claude is an expert at mak-ing them. He "nostalgically" remembers the days when he had to make scrambled eggs to order for customers of Chambrette's restaurant by stir-ring the eggs over a water bath for half an hour!

   ¾ cup (200 g) butter
   4 thick slices white bread, crusts removed, cut in triangles
   8 eggs
   Salt and pepper
   ⅓ cup (80 g) grated Gruyère cheese
   2 teaspoons chopped mixed tarragon, chervil and chives
   2 teaspoons Dijon-style mustard

Melt half the butter in a skillet and fry the slices of bread until golden brown on both sides. Drain well on paper towels.

Beat the eggs with salt and pepper until thoroughly mixed and frothy. Melt the remaining butter in a heavy-based saucepan, add the eggs and stir constantly over low heat with a wooden spoon until the mixture begins to thicken. Remove from the heat and stir in the cheese, chopped herbs and mustard. Pile onto a platter and surround with the bread. Serve at once.

Ham Cornets

CORNETS DE JAMBON

Be very careful when unmolding the cornets since they break easily. If they don't come out readily, run a small knife between the ham and the mold.

6 large (or 12 small) thin slices cooked ham
6 olives, halved and pitted
1 cup (125 g) diced carrot
1 cup (125 g) diced root celery or turnip
1 cup (125 g) shelled peas
1 cup (125 g) green beans, cut in ¼" (6 mm) lengths
Salt and pepper

For the Stiff Mayonnaise:
2 egg yolks
Salt and white pepper
2 tablespoons white wine vinegar
1 teaspoon Dijon-style mustard
1¼ cups (3 dl) oil
½ envelope (4 g) gelatin
¼ cup (6 cl) water

12 cornet molds
Pastry bag with small star tube

The recipe serves 6.

Trim any fat from the ham and cut large slices into two triangles. Shape the ham slices into cones and insert into the molds to line them; trim the tops level with the molds and chop the trimmings. So they are easy to fill, set the molds upright in a bowl of crushed ice, or tuck them in an egg carton.

Put the carrot and root celery or turnip in cold salted water, cover, bring to a boil and simmer 10–12 minutes or until just tender and drain thoroughly. Cook the peas and green beans in boiling salted water 5–8 minutes or until just tender, refresh with cold water and drain thoroughly.

For the stiff mayonnaise: In a small bowl beat the egg yolks with a little salt, pepper, 1 tablespoon vinegar and mustard until thick. Add the oil drop by drop, whisking constantly. When 2 tablespoons oil have been added, the mixture should be very thick. The remaining oil can be added a little more quickly. When all the oil has been added, stir in the remaining vinegar and taste for seasoning. Sprinkle the gelatin over the water in a small pan and let stand 5 minutes until spongy. Melt over low heat and stir into the mayonnaise. Reserve ¼ cup (6 cl) mayonnaise for decoration and stir the rest into the drained vegetables and ham trimmings. Taste for seasoning.

Fill the ham cornets with vegetable mixture, smooth the tops and chill 2 hours or until set. Spread the remaining mixture on a platter to form a 1" (2.5 cm) thick bed, smooth the edges, cover and chill. Cornets and salad can be prepared 8 hours before serving and kept in the refrigerator.

Not more than an hour before serving, unmold the cornets and arrange them, points to the center, on the vegetable mixture. Put the remaining mayonnaise in a pastry bag with a star tube and pipe rosettes on the cornets. Top each with an olive half. Serve chilled.

Terrine of Duck with Orange
TERRINE DE CANARD A L'ORANGE

This terrine should be delicately flavored with orange. After all, reminds Claude, it is duck terrine with orange and not orange terrine with duck.

> 1 pound (500 g) bacon, rind removed and thinly sliced,
>   or barding fat
> 5-5½ pound (2-2.5 kg) duck
> 3 tablespoons Grand Marnier
> 2 tablespoons brandy
> Salt and freshly ground black pepper
> 1 pound (500 g) pork, half fat and half lean
> 2 chicken livers and the duck liver
> 1 medium onion, quartered
> ½ teaspoon ground allspice
> 2 eggs
> Grated rind of 2 oranges
> 4 slices seedless navel orange (for garnish)

> **For the Luting Paste:**
> ⅓ cup (50 g) flour
> 2–3 tablespoons water

> *Terrine (2 quart or 2 L capacity) with tight-fitting lid*

> The recipe serves 10.

Line the terrine with overlapping bacon strips or barding fat, covering the bottom and sides of the mold. Reserve a few strips for the top. Set the oven at 350°F (175°C).

Remove the duck skin and discard or use it as additional lining for the terrine. Cut breast meat into large strips and marinate in Grand Marnier, brandy, salt and pepper for 1 hour. Cut away all other meat from the duck and grind it with the pork, livers and onion. Add the allspice, eggs, orange rind and marinade drained from the duck breast. Add plenty of salt and pepper. Sauté a teaspoon of the mixture to taste for seasoning.

Pack the terrine with layers of the ground meat mixture and the duck strips, beginning and ending with ground meat. Top with the remaining bacon strips and cover with the terrine lid. *For the luting paste:* Mix the flour and water and seal the gap between the lid and the mold with the paste.

Set the dish in a water bath and bring to a boil. Cook in preheated oven 1¼–1½ hours or until a skewer inserted in the terrine through the hole of the lid for 30 seconds is hot to the touch when withdrawn. Cool to tepid, uncover, set a plate and a 2 pound (1 kg) weight on top and chill. The terrine should be kept at least two days or up to a week in the refrigerator so the flavor mellows. It can also be frozen.

To finish: Discard the bacon slices from the top and scrape off any fat. Arrange the orange slices down the center.

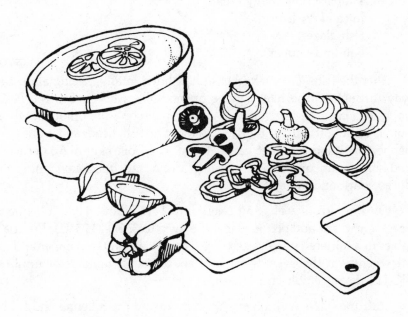

Sea Bass Fillets with Vegetable Julienne

SUPREMES DE BAR, JULIENNE DE LEGUMES

Claude often tells a student to fillet his fish quickly so it won't suffer.

4–5 pound (1.75–2.5 kg) sea bass with head and bones,
  yielding about 1½–2 pounds (750 g–1 kg) fillets
4–5 carrots
White part of 6 leeks
½ bunch celery
Salt and pepper
3 tablespoons (45 g) butter

For the Fish Glaze:
Head and bones of the fish
1 medium onion, sliced
1 tablespoon (15 g) butter
1 quart (1 L) water
10 peppercorns
Bouquet garni

For the White Wine Sauce:
2 shallots, finely chopped
1 cup (250 g) butter
½ cup (1.25 dl) white wine
1 tablespoon heavy cream
Juice of ½ lemon
Fish glaze
Salt and pepper

Fillet the fish. Cut each fillet in half horizontally, slicing almost all the way through so the fillet can be opened like a book. *Use the head and bones to make the fish glaze:* In a saucepan cook the onion slowly in the butter until soft but not brown. Add the fish head and bones, water, peppercorns and bouquet garni. Bring to a boil, skimming occasionally, and simmer uncovered 20 minutes. Strain and boil again until very reduced, dark and syrupy.

Cut the carrots, leeks and celery into 1½" (about 4 cm) julienne strips. Season with salt and pepper. Heat the oven to 350°F (175°C). Put the vegetables in a buttered pan or casserole, cover with buttered paper and the lid. Stew gently in the oven, stirring often, about 25 minutes or until tender. NOTE: the vegetables burn easily.

Stuff the fillets with a generous amount of the julienne and fold them closed. Reserve the remaining julienne. Place the fish in a steamer, season with salt and pepper and steam above boiling salted water 7–8 minutes or until barely tender. Arrange on a platter and keep warm.

For the white wine sauce: Cook the shallots slowly in 1 tablespoon of the butter. Add the wine and cook about 5 minutes or until reduced to 2 tablespoons. Add the cream and reduce again to 2 tablespoons. Beat in the remaining butter gradually in small pieces. Work sometimes over very low heat and sometimes off the heat, so that the butter softens and thickens the sauce without melting. Add the remaining vegetables, lemon juice, fish glaze, salt and pepper to taste. Pour over fillets and serve.

Provençal Scallops
COQUILLES ST. JACQUES A LA PROVENÇALE

Scallops should always be cooked briefly or they will be tough.

> 1 lemon
> 2 cloves garlic, finely chopped
> 2 shallots, finely chopped
> 2 tablespoons parsley
> ¼ cup (30 g) flour
> ¼ teaspoon salt
> Pinch of pepper
> 1½ pounds (750 g) scallops
> ¼ cup (60 g) butter

4–8 scallop shells—optional

As its name suggests, garlic is the predominant flavor of this dish. However, the amount can be adjusted to taste. The recipe serves 6–8 as a first course or 4 as a main course.

With a sharp or serrated knife, cut the pith and outer skin from the lemon. Cut the segments away from the skin and then cut the flesh in small dice. Mix with the garlic, shallots and parsley.

Mix the flour with salt and pepper. Discard the small membrane at the side of scallops. Toss scallops in the seasoned flour until coated. In a frying pan heat the butter until foaming, add the scallops and cook over high heat until browned, allowing 2-3 minutes on each side. **NOTE:** the scallops should not be crowded in the pan and may need to be cooked in two batches. If cooked too slowly, they will stew rather than brown. Transfer to a hot platter. Add the lemon mixture to the pan, sauté 1-2 minutes and pour over the scallops. Put in scallop shells or on a serving dish and serve.

Bouillabaisse
BOUILLABAISSE

Claude says you need an aquarium full of fish to make bouillabaisse.

3 pounds (1.5 kg) white fish such as monkfish, red mullet,
 whiting, bass, red snapper, perch, haddock, porgy or flounder
2 pounds (1 kg) rich fish such as conger eel, Moray eel
 or striped bass
2 large Dungeness crabs, or 8–10 small blue crabs—optional
1 large spiny lobster, or 8–10 small lobster tails—optional
2 medium onions, sliced
White part of 2 leeks, sliced
2 stalks celery, sliced
¾ cup (2 dl) olive oil
3 tomatoes, peeled, seeded and chopped
3–4 cloves garlic, crushed
Bouquet garni
Strip of orange rind
2 sprigs fresh fennel, or 1 teaspoon dried fennel
¼ teaspoon saffron
Salt and freshly ground black pepper
1 tablespoon tomato paste
1 tablespoon anise liquor (Pernod or Pastis)
¼ cup (30 g) chopped parsley (for sprinkling)

For the Marinade:
3 tablespoons olive oil
2 cloves garlic, finely chopped
Pinch of saffron

For the Croûtes:
1 long loaf of French bread, cut into about
 20 diagonal slices
½ cup (1.25 dl) olive oil
1 clove garlic, halved

The greater the variety of fish, the better the bouillabaisse will
be. Some white and some rich-fleshed fish should always be in-
cluded. The recipe serves 8–10.

Cut the fish in chunks, discarding skin and fins. Use the fish heads and
tails to make fish stock: barely cover with water, bring to a boil, simmer 15
minutes and strain. Meanwhile, marinate the fish in the olive oil, garlic and

saffron. Leave all shellfish in their shells; with a cleaver, chop large crabs and spiny lobster into pieces, discarding the stomach and intestinal veins of the lobster and the finger-like gills of the large crabs.

Sauté onions, leeks and celery in the oil in a large kettle until soft but not brown. Add the tomatoes, garlic, bouquet garni, orange rind, fennel and stock. Sprinkle in the saffron and add salt and pepper. Bring to a boil and simmer 30–45 minutes.

For the croûtes: Brown the sliced bread on both sides in the olive oil. Rub each croûte with garlic.

Twenty minutes before serving: Bring the liquid to a boil, uncovered, add the rich fish and shellfish and boil as hard as possible for 7 minutes. Shake the pan from time to time to prevent the mixture from sticking. Put the white fish on top and boil 8–10 minutes longer or until the fish just flake easily, adding more water if necessary to cover all the fish. NOTE: it is important to keep the liquid boiling fast so that the oil emulsifies with the broth and does not float on the surface.

Transfer the fish to a hot, deep platter and keep it warm. Whisk tomato paste and anise liquor into the broth and pour into a serving bowl or tureen. Sprinkle broth and fish with chopped parsley and serve at once. Broth, fish and croûtes are served separately and are combined by the diner, or the broth and croûtes may be eaten together and the fish afterwards.

Shellfish Quiche
QUICHE AUX FRUITS DE MER

*This quiche calls for raw shellfish, which give a good, fresh flavor. If no
raw shellfish are available, use cooked lobster or crabmeat.*

For the Pie Pastry:
1 cup (125 g) flour
¼ cup (60 g) unsalted butter
1 egg yolk
⅓ teaspoon (2 g) salt
3½–4 tablespoons cold water

For the Shellfish:
1 quart (1 L) fresh mussels
1 pound (500 g) raw scampi, in shells
7 ounces (200 g) raw shelled scallops

For the Custard:
1 egg
2 egg yolks
¼ cup (6 cl) milk
¾ cup (2 dl) heavy cream
Salt and pepper
Pinch of grated nutmeg
Shallow 8–9" (20–23 cm) pie or tart pan or flan ring

The recipe serves 6–8.

Make the pie pastry (see **Normandy Pear Pie**) and chill 30 minutes.

Set the oven at 400°F (200°C). Lightly butter the pan or ring. Line it
with the dough and chill until firm. Prick the base with a fork. Line the
dough with brown or waxed paper, pressing it well into the base, fill with
uncooked beans or rice and bake 10–12 minutes until the pastry is set and
beginning to brown. Remove the paper and beans and bake the shell 7–10
minutes more or until lightly browned. Remove from the oven and let the
shell cool slightly. Lower the oven temperature to 375°F (190°C).

For the shellfish: Scrape the mussels clean and wash thoroughly. Cook
in a covered saucepan over high heat, tossing occasionally, about 5
minutes or just until open. Discard any that do not open. Shell the mussels
and remove the string-like part surrounding each one. Shell the scampi and
cut in 4–5 pieces. Slice each scallop diagonally in 2–3 slices. Arrange the
scallops, scampi and mussels in pie shell and season lightly.

For the custard: beat together the egg, yolks, milk and cream until smooth; season well with salt, pepper and nutmeg.

Add the custard to the pie shell, filling it three-quarters full, and bake in preheated oven. After about 15 minutes or when partly set, add more custard to completely fill the shell. Bake all together 25–30 minutes or until set and browned. NOTE: do not overcook or the custard will curdle. The custard puffs during baking but shrinks slightly when taken from the oven. Serve hot or cool but not chilled.

This pie can be made a day ahead but the pastry becomes soggy on standing too long. Keep tightly covered in the refrigerator and reheat in a 350°F (175°C) oven, taking care the filling does not curdle from overcooking.

Turban of Sole
TURBAN DE SOLE

When asked in a demonstration why he drops the filled mold on the counter a few times, Claude says it's to wake up the audience. Actually, it makes the filling more compact and knocks out air holes.

8 sole fillets (about 1½ pounds or 750 g)
8–16 cooked, peeled shrimps—optional
1 canned truffle, drained and thinly sliced (for garnish)
   —optional
6 large, cooked unpeeled shrimps (for garnish)

For the Filling:
3 whole whiting (total weight 2½–3 pounds or 1.2–1.5 kg),
   or 1 pound (500 g) fillets
⅓ cup (100 g) butter, softened
2 egg yolks
Salt and pepper
Pinch of grated nutmeg
Pinch of cayenne
1 egg white
⅔ cup (2 dl) heavy cream

For the White Butter Sauce:
3 tablespoons white wine vinegar
3 tablespoons dry white wine
2 shallots, very finely chopped
1 cup (250 g) butter, very cold
Salt and white pepper

Ring mold (1 quart or 1 L capacity)

Haddock or flounder can replace whiting in the filling. The recipe serves 6.

For the filling: If using whole fish, remove the fillets from the bone and skin them. Purée the fish in an electric food processor. Add the butter and egg yolks and continue to process. Alternatively, work the fish twice through the fine plate of a grinder, then work in the butter and yolks in a blender. If possible, also work the mixture through a fine drum sieve. Put into a metal bowl set in a pan of ice water. Add salt, pepper, nutmeg and cayenne. With a wooden spoon, beat in the egg white. Gradually beat in the cream and taste again for seasoning.

Set the oven at 350°F (175°C) and butter the mold. With the flat part of a heavy knife or cleaver pound the sole fillets between two pieces of waxed paper. Halve each fillet crosswise, cutting diagonally. Line the mold, putting the white side of each fillet downwards, the broad end to the outside and leaving the tail end hanging into the center. Overlap the fillets slightly at the broad end. If you like, put peeled shrimps between the fillets near the tail ends. Spoon the filling into the mold and fold the fillet ends over it. Cover the mold with buttered foil; set in a water bath and bring to a boil on top of the stove. Put in the oven and cook 30–35 minutes or until firm to the touch. Let sit for 10 minutes. Tip the mold sideways to drain off any excess liquid. The mold can be assembled 3–4 hours ahead and cooked just before serving.

For the white butter sauce: In a small saucepan (not aluminum) boil the wine vinegar, wine and shallots until reduced to 2 tablespoons. Set the pan over low heat and whisk in the butter gradually in small pieces to make a smooth, creamy sauce. Once in a while, remove from the heat. The butter should soften and thicken the sauce without melting. Season with salt and white pepper.

To finish: Heat the large shrimps by dropping them in boiling salted water, bringing them just back to a boil and draining. Unmold the turban on a heated platter. Wipe away any liquid with paper towels, coat the mold with sauce, top it with sliced truffles and arrange the shrimps around the edge. Serve the remaining sauce separately.

Chicken Breasts with Port
SUPREMES DE VOLAILLE AU PORTO

A suprême is the boneless breast from one side of a chicken. The first wing bone may be cut off or left attached. Claude removes the suprêmes from a chicken with amazing speed, but if it's your first try, allow plenty of time.

> 4 chicken suprêmes
> Salt and freshly ground black pepper
> 6 tablespoons (50 g) flour
> 6 tablespoons (90 g) butter
> ¼ cup (6 cl) port
>
> **For the Basic Brown Sauce:**
> 1 cup (2.5 dl) well-flavored brown stock
> 2 teaspoons arrowroot or potato starch
> 1 tablespoon cold water

For the basic brown sauce: Bring the stock to a boil. Mix the arrowroot or potato starch to a paste with the cold water. Add gradually to the stock, whisking constantly, until just thick enough to coat a spoon.

About 20 minutes before serving: Season the suprêmes and coat with flour, patting off the excess. Heat 4 tablespoons (60 g) butter and fry the suprêmes 5–6 minutes on each side until golden brown and tender. Keep warm until ready to serve.

For the sauce: Discard the fat from frying the suprêmes, add the port and brown sauce and bring to a boil, stirring to deglaze the juices. Strain the sauce, taste for seasoning and whisk in the remaining 2 tablespoons (30 g) butter in small pices. NOTE: do not reheat or it will separate.

To serve: Arrange the chicken suprêmes on a platter. Spoon some sauce over each and serve the rest separately.

Stuffed Veal Breast
POITRINE DE VEAU FARCIE

Sometimes Claude uses more eggs and leaves them whole; when the veal is cut there is a bull's-eye of egg in the center of each slice.

3–3½ pound (1.3–1.5 kg) piece of breast of veal
Salt and pepper
1 tablespoon oil
2 tablespoons (30 g) butter
1 medium onion, quartered
1 carrot, quartered
1 stalk celery, cut in 2" (5 cm) lengths
1 cup (2.5 dl) white wine
1½ cups (3.75 dl) veal stock
1 clove garlic, crushed
Bouquet garni

For the Stuffing:
1 onion, finely chopped
2 tablespoons (30 g) butter
1 pound (500 g) veal, ground
1 cup (50 g) fresh white breadcrumbs
2 cloves garlic, finely chopped
Grated rind of 1 lemon
2 tablespoons chopped parsley
Pinch of grated nutmeg
Salt and freshly ground black pepper
2 eggs, beaten to mix
2 hard-cooked eggs, sliced
2 ounces (60 g) cooked ham, cut in julienne strips

The recipe serves 6.

For the stuffing: Cook the onion slowly in the butter until soft but not brown. Stir into the ground veal with the breadcrumbs, garlic, lemon rind, parsley, nutmeg and plenty of salt and pepper. Stir in the beaten eggs and beat the stuffing well. Sauté a teaspoon of stuffing in a little oil and taste for seasoning. Preheat the oven to 350°F (175°C).

Bone the veal breast and spread it, fat side down, on a board; reserve the bones. Season the veal. Spread the stuffing over the meat, leaving a 1" (2.5 cm) border, and top with the sliced eggs. Scatter ham strips over the eggs, roll the veal and tie neatly in a cylinder.

In a casserole brown the veal in oil and butter. Remove the meat, add the onion, carrot and celery, cover and cook gently 5–7 minutes until softened. Add the bones, set the meat on top and add the wine, stock, garlic, bouquet garni and salt and pepper. Bring to a boil on top of the stove and braise in the heated oven 2–2½ hours or until tender. Remove the meat from the pan, boil the cooking liquid until reduced to about 1½ cups (3.75 dl), strain and skim off any fat. Taste for seasoning.

The veal may be served hot or cold. The cooking juices may be used warm as a sauce or chilled, jelled and chopped as a garnish for the cold meat.

Beef Stroganoff
BOEUF STROGANOFF

For this recipe the head and tail of the beef fillet are often used. It can be cooked in a chafing dish at the table, providing the burner gives a strong heat.

> ⅓ cup (85 g) butter
> 1 onion, sliced
> ½ pound (250 g) mushrooms, sliced
> 1½ pound (750 g) beef fillet, cut in 2″x³/₈″x³/₈″
>   (5x1x1 cm) strips
> 1 tablespoon paprika—optional
> ¼ cup (6 cl) brandy
> Salt and freshly ground black pepper
> 1 cup (2.5 dl) sour cream

In a skillet or chafing dish, melt 2 tablespoons (30 g) butter and cook the onions over medium heat until golden brown. Add the mushrooms and cook, stirring, until tender. Take them out and wipe out the pan.

If you like, roll the beef strips in paprika. Melt half the remaining butter and fry a few strips of the steak over high heat for 1–2 minutes, stirring occasionally so they brown on the outside and remain rare in the center. NOTE: if the pan is not hot enough, or too much steak is cooked at once, the meat will stew rather than brown. Take out the browned steak and fry the rest in small quantities, adding more butter when the pan is dry.

Return the meat to the pan, heat well, pour over the brandy and flame. Add the onions, mushrooms, salt and pepper and cook 1–2 minutes until very hot. Add the sour cream, bring almost to a boil, taste for seasoning and serve. NOTE: if the sour cream is boiled, it will separate.

Pork Chops Dijonnaise

COTES DE PORC DIJONNAISE

When lean bacon is not available, Canadian bacon is an excellent alternative. Veal chops can be prepared in the same way.

1 tablespoon oil
⅓ pound (150 g) piece lean bacon, cut in dice (lardons)
18 small onions, scalded and peeled
4 large pork chops
1 tablespoon (7 g) flour
½ cup (1.25 dl) white wine
1 cup (2.5 dl) veal or chicken stock
Bouquet garni
Salt and pepper
¼ cup (6 cl) heavy cream
2 tablespoons Dijon-style mustard, or to taste
1 tablespoon chopped parsley

In a large skillet heat the oil, add the bacon and cook, stirring occasionally, until browned and most of the fat is extracted. Take out, add the onions and brown them also. Take them out, add the chops and brown on both sides. Take them out and discard all but 2 tablespoons (30 g) fat. Sprinkle in the flour and cook until bubbling. Add the wine, stock, bouquet garni, salt and pepper and bring to a boil, stirring.

Replace the chops and bacon, cover and simmer on top of the stove or in a 350°F (175°C) oven for 25–30 minutes. Add the onions and continue cooking for 15 minutes or until chops and onions are tender. The chops can be cooked up to 48 hours ahead and kept in the refrigerator, or they can be frozen.

To finish: Reheat the chops on top of the stove, if necessary, arrange them overlapping on a platter and keep warm. If necessary, boil the sauce to reduce it until well-flavored. Add the cream, bring just back to the boil, take from the heat and stir in the mustard. NOTE: add mustard at the last minute and do not boil as the flavor turns bitter. Discard bouquet garni, taste for seasoning and spoon the sauce and garnish over the chops. Sprinkle with chopped parsley and serve.

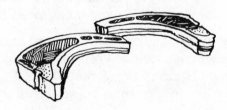

Crown Roast of Lamb

CARRE D'AGNEAU EN COURONNE

Watch carefully as Claude "turns" vegetables to give them all a perfect oval shape. Besides being attractive, uniformly shaped vegetables cook evenly.

3–4 tablespoons oil
3 racks of lamb (rib sections)
Salt and freshly ground black pepper
1 cup (2.5 dl) white wine
2 cups (5 dl) beef or veal stock

For the Garnish:
2 pounds (1 kg) baby carrots, peeled,
  or large carrots, peeled and quartered
2 pounds (1 kg) small new potatoes, peeled,
  or 4 large potatoes, peeled and quartered
2 teaspoons sugar
¾ cup (175 g) butter
Salt and pepper
2 pounds (1 kg) baby Brussels sprouts or green beans, cooked

The recipe serves 8–10.

On the stove heat the oil in a large roasting pan and quickly sear the fat side of each rack. Tie into a crown roast, season and return to the roasting pan. Preheat the oven to 400°F (200°C).

For the garnish: To make a particularly attractive garnish, you might trim the carrots and potatoes into olive shapes. Bring the carrots to a boil with the sugar, 2 tablespoons (30 g) butter, salt, pepper and water to cover. Simmer 10–15 minutes or until tender. Boil rapidly until nearly all the liquid has evaporated to form a shiny glaze. In a sauté pan or shallow casserole melt ⅓ cup (100 g) butter and put in the potatoes in one layer. Cover and cook over high heat, shaking the pan occasionally, 15–20 minutes or until tender. Sprinkle with salt and pepper. Before serving, reheat the sprouts or beans in the remaining butter and season.

Roast the lamb 15–20 minutes or until a meat thermometer registers 140°F (60°C) for rare or 160°F (70°C) for medium done meat. Discard the strings, transfer the meat to a platter and keep warm. Discard the fat, pour in white wine and stock and deglaze the pan, boiling until the gravy is well reduced. Taste for seasoning and strain into a sauceboat. Reheat the vegetables if necessary and pile into the center of the crown. Decorate the platter with any remaining vegetables and top each chop bone with a paper frill.

Cucumber Gratin

CONCOMBRES AU GRATIN

If trimming the cucumber pieces to olive shapes, remove as many of the seeds as possible.

3 large cucumbers (about 2 pounds or 1 kg)
3 tablespoons (45 g) butter
Salt and pepper
1 tablespoon water
2 tablespoons (15 g) grated Gruyère or Parmesan cheese
   (for sprinkling)

For the Mornay Sauce:
1–1¼ cups (2.5–3 dl) milk
1 tablespoon (15 g) butter
1½ tablespoons (10 g) flour
Salt and pepper
Pinch of grated nutmeg
1 egg yolk
¼ cup (30 g) grated Gruyère or Parmesan cheese

Peel the cucumbers. Either cut them in 2″ (5 cm) lengths, divide each in four lengthwise and trim the pieces to olive shapes, or cut in half lengthwise, scoop out the seeds and slice into crescents. In a sauté pan melt 2 tablespoons (30 g) of the butter and add the cucumbers, salt, pepper and water. Cover and cook over low heat, shaking occasionally, 5–7 minutes or until nearly tender.

For the Mornay sauce: Scald the milk. In a heavy-based saucepan melt the butter, whisk in the flour and cook 1–2 minutes until foaming but not browned; let cool. Add the hot milk, whisk well, then bring the sauce to a boil, whisking constantly, and add a little salt, pepper and nutmeg to taste. Simmer 3–5 minutes. Remove from heat and beat in the egg yolk and cheese. Taste for seasoning. The sauce should just coat a spoon; if it is too thick, stir in up to ¼ cup (6 cl) more milk.

Spoon a little sauce into a buttered, shallow baking dish, add the cucumber pieces and coat with the remaining sauce. Sprinkle with 2 tablespoons (15 g) grated cheese. Melt the remaining butter and sprinkle on top. The dish can be prepared up to 24 hours ahead, but the cucumbers should be undercooked to allow for reheating. Keep covered in the refrigerator.

To finish: If the cucumbers are still warm, brown under the broiler. If cold, reheat in a 400°F (200°C) oven 10–12 minutes until browned.

Stuffed Eggplant Imam Bayeldi
AUBERGINES FARCIES IMAM BAYELDI

Imam bayeldi means fainting imam, but no one knows whether he fainted from pleasure at the richness of this dish or from horror at its cost. (Olive oil was a valuable Mediterranean commodity sometimes used for barter.)

2 medium eggplants, or 4 baby eggplants, unpeeled
Salt and freshly ground black pepper
½ cup (1.25 dl) olive oil
5 ripe tomatoes, peeled
3 medium onions, chopped
2 cloves garlic, chopped
2 tablespoons chopped parsley

Heat the oven to 425°F (220°C). Cut the stems from the eggplants and halve them lengthwise. With the tip of a knife, cut around the edge inside the skin; slash the center. Sprinkle the cut surfaces with salt and leave 30 minutes to draw out the bitter juices. Wipe with paper towels. Put in an oiled baking dish, pour on 4 tablespoons (6 cl) olive oil and bake in preheated oven 20–25 minutes or until tender. Remove from the oven, gently scoop out the flesh and chop it, reserving the shells.

Seed and chop 3 tomatoes; slice the others. Heat 3 tablespoons oil and sauté the onions until golden brown. Add the garlic and cook 1 minute; then take from the heat and stir in the chopped tomatoes, salt and pepper. Cook 15 minutes or until much of the liquid has evaporated. Stir in the eggplant pulp and cook 3–4 more minutes. Take from the heat, add chopped parsley and taste for seasoning.

Season the eggplant shells and return to the baking dish. Spoon in the filling and stick in 3 or 4 tomato slices at an angle at regular intervals. Pour on the remaining 1 tablespoon oil and bake in the oven 15–20 minutes or until the filling is hot. Serve hot or at room temperature. The eggplants can be kept 2–3 days covered in the refrigerator, and they reheat well.

Tourte of Green Vegetables

TOURTE DE LEGUMES VERTS

This tourte is a kind of quiche without pastry; the vegetables are baked in a rich custard filling. You may vary the vegetables in the filling by adding sautéed zucchini slices or blanched cauliflower flowerets. All the vegetables can be cooked up to 24 hours ahead and kept in the refrigerator.

1 head cabbage
Salt and pepper
5 leeks (about 1 pound or 500 g)
½ pound (250 g) green beans
2 tablespoons (30 g) butter
¼ pound (125 g) mushrooms, sliced

For the Custard:
2 eggs
2 egg yolks
½ cup (1.25 dl) milk
1½ cups (3.75 dl) heavy cream
Salt and pepper
Pinch of grated nutmeg

9" (23 cm) layer pan or moule à manqué

Remove the large ribs from the cabbage leaves and wash the leaves well. Place in a large pan of boiling salted water, bring back to a boil and boil 7–8 minutes or until just tender. Refresh under cold running water and drain thoroughly. Dry well. Thoroughly clean the leeks, sprinkle with salt and steam above boiling water for 15–20 minutes or until barely tender but still slightly crunchy. Refresh under cold running water, drain and gently squeeze out excess moisture. Cut in 1" (2.5 cm) lengths. Cook the green beans in a large pan of boiling salted water 7–10 minutes or until just tender. Refresh under cold running water and drain thoroughly. Cut them in thirds. In a frying pan or skillet heat the butter, add the sliced mushrooms, salt and pepper and sauté over high heat, tossing often, 3–4 minutes or until tender and lightly browned.

For the custard: Beat together the eggs, yolks, milk and heavy cream until smooth. Season well with salt, pepper and nutmeg.

Heat a baking sheet in a 350°F (175°C) oven. *To assemble the tourte:* Butter the mold, line the bottom with a buttered circle of parchment paper and then line the bottom and sides with cabbage leaves, leaving them hanging over the sides of the mold. Chop the remaining leaves. Arrange a layer of sautéed mushrooms in the lined pan. Top with a layer of leeks, then a layer of green beans, last a layer of chopped cabbage. Season each layer. Continue until the mold is full. Pour in enough of the custard to come to the top of the vegetables. Fold the overhanging leaves back so they cover the custard.

Bake on the hot baking sheet in preheated oven about 45–55 minutes or until the filling is dry when tested with a knife. Let set for a few minutes and unmold. Serve hot or at room temperature.

Spinach Mold

PAIN D'EPINARDS

As a variation, carrot and cauliflower purées can be layered with the spinach to give three-colored molds.

1½ pounds (750 g) fresh spinach
Salt and pepper
3 tablespoons (45 g) butter
¾ cup (40 g) fresh white breadcrumbs
1½ cups (3.75 dl) hot milk
2 eggs, beaten to mix
1 egg yolk
Pinch of grated nutmeg
Mornay sauce (see **Cucumber Gratin**)

Plain or charlotte mold (3–4 cup or 7.5 dl–1 L capacity),
*   or 4 custard cups (each 1 cup or 2.5 dl capacity)*

This mold can also be made with two 10-ounce (300 g) packages of frozen spinach, but cook it very briefly and do not line the mold with spinach leaves.

Remove spinach stems, wash the leaves well and blanch 12–14 large leaves in boiling water for 1 minute. Drain on paper towels and leave whole. Cook the remaining spinach in boiling salted water for 5 minutes or until tender. Drain thoroughly, refresh with cold water, squeeze thoroughly to remove all the water and chop.

Butter the mold or cups and line with the blanched leaves. Melt the butter, add the chopped spinach and cook 3–4 minutes, stirring, until all moisture has evaporated. Remove from the heat. Soak the breadcrumbs in the hot milk for 5 minutes and add to the spinach with the eggs, yolk, nutmeg and seasoning. Spoon the mixture into the lined mold or cups and cover with buttered foil. The spinach molds can be prepared 6–8 hours ahead; keep covered in the refrigerator.

Three-quarters to one hour before serving: Set the oven at 350°F (175°C). Stand the mold or cups in a pan of hot water and bring the water just to a boil on top of the stove. Bake in preheated oven, allowing 45–55 minutes for the mold or 20–25 minutes for the cups, or until firm. Lift the mold from the water bath and let cool slightly before unmolding onto a platter. Spoon some of the sauce around the spinach mold and serve the rest separately.

Braised Celery
CELERIS BRAISES

It's a good idea to remove the tough celery strings with a vegetable peeler.

> 1 bunch of celery
> 1 tablespoon oil
> 2–3 slices bacon, diced—optional
> 1 onion, diced
> 1 carrot, diced
> About 1 cup (2.5 dl) white veal stock
> Bouquet garni
> Salt and pepper
> 1 teaspoon arrowroot or potato starch
> 1 tablespoon water
> 1 tablespoon chopped parsley

Wash the celery and cut in 3″ (7.5 cm) lengths, discarding the leaves. Blanch in boiling water for 1 minute and drain. Tie in small bundles with string. Set the oven at 350°F (175°C).

In a sauté pan or casserole, heat the oil and fry the bacon until the fat runs. Add the onion and carrot and cook over low heat 5–7 minutes until soft. Put the celery on top and add the stock, bouquet garni, salt and pepper. NOTE: if using bacon, salt may not be needed. Cover and braise in preheated oven for ¾–1 hour or until the celery is tender. Add more stock during cooking if the pan gets dry. The celery can be cooked 1–2 days ahead and kept in the refrigerator.

Reheat celery mixture if necessary on top of the stove. Transfer the celery to a platter, remove strings and keep warm. Strain the cooking liquid into a pan and reduce if necessary to about ¾ cup (2 dl). Mix the arrowroot and water to a paste. Stir in enough of the arrowroot paste to thicken the mixture slightly and taste for seasoning. Spoon over the celery, sprinkle with parsley and serve.

Souffléd Oranges
ORANGES SOUFFLEES

It's important that egg whites used in soufflés be very stiff and smooth. Claude prefers to beat them in a copper bowl, and when students ask how long to beat, he answers, "until you're very tired."

4 large navel oranges
1 cup (2.5 dl) milk
3 egg yolks
Grated rind of 1 orange
¼ cup (60 g) sugar
2½ tablespoons (20 g) flour
3 tablespoons Grand Marnier or other orange liqueur
1 teaspoon vanilla extract
5 egg whites
Confectioners' sugar (for sprinkling)

Pastry bag with large star tube—optional

Cut the whole oranges in half crosswise. Scoop out the flesh without piercing the rind. Scald the milk. Beat the yolks, orange rind and half the sugar until thick; stir in the flour. Pour on the boiling milk, whisking, and return the mixture to the saucepan. Bring to a boil, whisking, and simmer 2 minutes. Take from the heat and stir in the Grand Marnier and vanilla. This soufflé base can be prepared 3–4 hours ahead. Rub the surface of the mixture with butter to prevent the formation of a skin and keep at room temperature.

Half an hour before serving: Set the oven at 400°F (200°C) and heat the soufflé base until very hot but not boiling. Whip the egg whites until stiff, add the remaining sugar and continue beating until glossy. Stir one-quarter of the whites into the orange mixture; then add this to the remaining whites and fold together as lightly as possible. Use the pastry bag with star tube to fill the orange halves or spoon the mixture into them. Bake in preheated oven 5 minutes or until puffed and brown. Sprinkle heavily with confectioners' sugar and return to the oven for 2 minutes. Serve at once.

Snow Eggs
OEUFS A LA NEIGE

If you overcook the custard, warns Claude, you'll end up with sweet scrambled eggs.

>2 cups (5 dl) milk
>Vanilla bean, split
>3–5 tablespoons (45–75 g) sugar
>4 egg yolks
>
>**For the Meringue "Eggs":**
>4 egg whites
>⅔ cup (125 g) sugar
>
>**For the Caramel:**
>⅓ cup (75 g) sugar
>3 tablespoons water

For the meringue: Whip the egg whites until stiff. Add 2 tablespoons (30 g) sugar and continue whisking 1 minute or until the mixture forms long peaks when the whisk is lifted. Fold in the remaining sugar.

To poach the "eggs": In a sauté pan or shallow saucepan bring the milk almost to a boil with the vanilla bean. Dip a large metal spoon into the milk, then shape an oval of meringue. Tap the handle of the spoon sharply on the sauté pan to detach the meringue. Add 4–5 "eggs" to the milk and poach them 30 seconds or until firm, turning them once. Lift out with a slotted spoon and drain on paper towels. Continue with the remaining meringue. NOTE: the "eggs" are lighter, but less creamy, if poached in water instead of milk, but the custard sauce must be made with milk.

For the custard sauce: Use 3 tablespoons (45 g) sugar if the "eggs" were cooked in milk, and 5 tablespoons (75 g) sugar if they were cooked in water. Strain the milk into a fairly deep saucepan and bring it almost to a boil. Beat the yolks with the sugar until thick and light. Whisk in half the hot milk and whisk the mixture back into the remaining milk. Heat gently, stirring constantly, until the custard thickens slightly; if you draw your finger across the back of the spoon it will leave a clear trail. Do not overcook or boil or the custard will curdle. Strain into a serving bowl.

To assemble: When the custard is cool, pile the meringue "eggs" in the center. *For the caramel:* Heat the sugar and water over low heat until dissolved; then boil steadily to a golden caramel that is not too dark. Let cool until it stops bubbling, then dribble it in criss-cross trails across the "eggs." The dessert can be made up to 4 hours ahead; keep in the refrigerator.

Caramel-Glazed Puffs

SALAMBOS

Salambôs are easier to make than éclairs because caramel repaces the usual fondant, which is difficult to make and to use.

For the Choux Pastry:
⅔ cup (110 g) flour
⅔ cup (1.8 dl) water
¼ teaspoon (1 g) salt
⅓ cup (75 g) unsalted butter
3–4 eggs
1 egg beaten with ½ teaspoon salt (for glaze)

For the Pastry Cream:
2 cups (5 dl) milk
6 egg yolks
½ cup (125 g) sugar
6 tablespoons (50 g) flour
1–2 tablespoons kirsch or rum

For the Topping:
¾ cup (150 g) sugar
¼ cup (6 cl) water
2 tablespoons blanched pistachios, finely chopped

Pastry bag with ½" (1.25 cm) and ¼" (6 mm) plain tubes

The recipe makes about 20 Salambôs.

Set the oven at 400°F (200°C). *For the choux pastry:* Sift the flour. In a saucepan heat the water, salt and butter until the butter is melted; then bring just to a boil and take from the heat. Immediately add all the flour and beat vigorously with a wooden spoon for a few seconds until the mixture is smooth and pulls away from the pan. Beat ½ to 1 minute over low heat to dry the mixture. Set aside one egg and beat it. Beat the remaining eggs into the dough, one by one. Beat in enough of the reserved egg to make a mixture that is very shiny and just falls from the spoon.

Put the dough into a pastry bag fitted with a ½" (1.25 cm) plain tube and pipe 1½" (3.75 cm) ovals well apart onto a baking sheet, or shape the ovals with a tablespoon. Brush with egg glaze and mark with a fork. If using an unventilated electric oven, prop open the door slightly. Bake

20–25 minutes or until the puffs are firm and brown. Transfer to a rack to cool. The puffs can be kept overnight in an airtight container, but they are at their best eaten within a few hours.

For the pastry cream: Scald the milk. Beat the yolks with the sugar until thick. Stir in the flour. Whisk the boiling milk into the yolk mixture, blend, return to the pan and whisk over low heat until boiling. Cook gently, whisking constantly, 2 minutes. Flavor with kirsch or rum and rub a piece of butter on top to prevent the formation of a skin. Stir the cream from time to time as it cools.

For the caramel topping: Heat the sugar with the water until dissolved; then boil without stirring to a light golden caramel. Plunge the base of the pan into a bowl of warm water to stop cooking. At once dip the top of each choux puff into the caramel and immediately sprinkle with a pinch of chopped pistachios. If the caramel sets before all are coated, warm it gently but do not cook it further. The pastry cream can be made and the puffs can be coated 4–5 hours before serving. Keep the puffs in a dry place.

Not more than 2 hours before serving: Put the pastry cream into a pastry bag fitted with a ¼″ (6 mm) plain tube. Make a slit in the side of each puff and fill with pastry cream.

Normandy Pear Pie
TARTE NORMANDE AUX POIRES

Although this pie is Norman in origin, now the beautiful pears from Claude's native Loire valley are often used to make it.

3–4 ripe pears
Granulated sugar (for sprinkling)
½ cup (1.25 dl) apricot jam glaze

For the Pie Pastry:
1½ cups (200 g) flour
⅓ cup (100 g) unsalted butter
1 egg yolk
½ teaspoon (3 g) salt
4–5 tablespoons cold water

For the Frangipane:
⅓ cup (100 g) butter
½ cup (100 g) sugar
1 egg, beaten to mix
1 egg yolk
2 teaspoons kirsch
¾ cup (100 g) blanched almonds, ground
2 tablespoons (15 g) flour

10-11" (25-27 cm) pie or tart pan

The recipe serves 8–10

For the pie pastry: Sift the flour onto a working surface and make a well in the center. Pound the butter to soften slightly. Place butter, yolk, salt and 4 tablespoons water in the well and work together with the fingertips until partly mixed. Gradually work in the flour, pulling the dough into large crumbs. If the crumbs are dry, sprinkle with a little more water. Press the dough firmly together. Work it by pushing it away with the heel of the hand and gathering it up with a dough scraper until smooth and pliable. Press into a ball, wrap and chill at least 30 minutes. Roll out the dough, line the pan, prick lightly with a fork, flute the edges and chill again until firm. Preheat the oven to 400°F (200°C).

For the frangipane: Cream the butter, gradually beat in the sugar and continue beating until light and soft. Gradually add the egg and yolk, beating well after each addition. Add the kirsch, then stir in the ground almonds and flour. Spoon into the pastry shell.

Peel, halve and core the pears. Cut crosswise in very thin slices and arrange pear halves on the frangipane in a wheel pattern, spreading the slices of each pear somewhat but maintaining the shape of the pear. Press them down gently until they touch the pastry dough base.

Bake in the bottom third of the oven 10–15 minutes until the dough is beginning to brown. Reduce heat to 350°F (175°C) and continue baking 10 minutes. Sprinkle with granulated sugar and continue cooking until the sugar melts and caramelizes slightly, the pears are tender and the frangipane is set. A short time before serving, brush the pie with melted apricot jam glaze. Serve at room temperature.

Normandy Pear Pie is best eaten the day it is baked, but it can be frozen. Just before serving, reheat to tepid in a 300°F (150°C) oven and brush with apricot jam glaze.

ANNE
WILLAN

Most people would tire from simply following Anne Willan around for a day—and would be exhausted after a week in her footsteps. At twenty-one she graduated from Cambridge with a master's degree in economics. A year later, in 1960, she had completed the most advanced course at London's Cordon Bleu Cookery School and was offered a post as teacher and demonstrator, which she filled for two years. Then it was on to the Paris Ecole du Cordon Bleu for a year to earn its *grand diplôme.* This was followed by more teaching as well as catering and a job as entertainment advisor at the Château de Versailles. Her next move was to the United States, where she worked first as an associate editor of *Gourmet Magazine* and later as food editor for the *Washington Star* and became an American citizen.

In 1975, having returned to Paris, Anne opened France's first bilingual cooking school—La Varenne. With her indefatigable spirit presiding, l'Ecole de Cuisine La Varenne flourishes, giving the lie to all the raised French eyebrows that once expressed doubt at the very idea of an Anglo/American, and a female at that, daring to start a serious cooking school on hallowed ground. Now the very chefs who may have scoffed accept invitations to give guest demonstrations at the school.

Anne breezes through the kitchens of the school noting everything. "That soufflé mixture is just the right consistency. It will rise," she says, commending a student from across the room. She seems to keep track of everything at La Varenne from the French accounting system to the state of the herbs in the window boxes.

A journalist and a superb, incredibly informed teacher, Anne is also an author. She was editor-in-chief of the twenty volume *Grand Diplôme Cooking Course.* Her own first book, *Entertaining Menus,* was published in 1974, followed by *Great Cooks and their Recipes* in 1977. Several more books are under way as are plans for demonstration tours in Europe and the United States. Anne is married and bringing up two young children as well. She explains her ability to accomplish so much: "I'm fortunate enough to be a part of two marvelous teams—one at home and one at work."

ANNE WILLAN

Appetizers
Rich Cheese Soufflé
Country Ham Pâté
Shrimp Pâté

Main Courses
Fish Fricassée with Limes and Ginger
Shrimp Newburg
Chicken and Shrimp Sauté à l'Indienne
Chicken Fricassée with Mushrooms and Baby Onions
Duck Steak with Green Peppercorns
Duck Ragoût with Madeira
Beef Fillet Cherniavsky
Veal Escalopes with Roquefort
Shoulder of Lamb à la Turque

Vegtables and Salads
Provençal Tomatoes
Eggplant Terrine
Potatoes Darphin
Baked Zucchini
Duck Skin and Liver Salad

Desserts
Peaches or Strawberries Cardinal
Strawberry Charlotte Malakoff
Chocolate Snowball
Hot Lemon Soufflé
Iced Coffee Soufflé
Trifle

Rich Cheese Soufflé

SOUFFLE RICHE AU FROMAGE

This recipe is risky as only a small amount of potato starch is used to stabilize the cream, cheese and butter. But the result is spectacular— the lightest imaginable cheese puff. Anne enhances the soufflé by putting diced lobster or shrimps, marinated in a very little cognac, in the dish before cooking.

> 1 cup (2.5 dl) heavy cream
> 1 tablespoon (10 g) potato starch
> 1 tablespoon (15 g) butter
> 5 egg yolks
> ½ cup (60 g) grated Parmesan cheese
> ½ cup (60 g) grated Gruyère cheese
> Salt and pepper
> Pinch of dry mustard
> 8 egg whites
>
> *1½ quart (1.5 L) soufflé dish*
>
> The recipe serves 4–6.

Butter the soufflé dish generously. In a heavy saucepan put the cream, potato starch and butter and heat gently, stirring, until the sauce thickens. Take at once from the heat or the sauce will separate. Stir in the egg yolks and cheeses, reserving 2 tablespoons (15 g) of the Gruyère to sprinkle on top of the soufflé. Heat gently, stirring until the mixture thickens slightly again. Do not overcook it, or the cheese will form strings. Take from the heat and add salt, pepper and mustard. The mixture should be highly seasoned to compensate for the blandness of the egg whites. The soufflé base can be prepared up to 3 hours ahead; keep the mixture covered with wet waxed paper to prevent the formation of a skin.

To finish the soufflé: Set the oven at 425°F (220°C). Beat the egg whites until stiff, if possible using a copper bowl. Heat the cheese mixture until hot to the touch. NOTE: do not let it cook into strings. Add about a quarter of the egg whites and stir until well mixed. Add this to the remaining egg whites and fold together as lightly as possible. Pour into the prepared soufflé dish, sprinkle with the remaining 2 tablespoons cheese and bake in the heated oven 12–15 minutes or until the soufflé is puffed and brown. Serve at once.

Country Ham Pâté

PATE DE CAMPAGNE AU JAMBON

Like all pâtés, this benefits from being kept at least 2–3 days before serving, so the flavor mellows.

½ pound (250 g) sliced barding fat or mild bacon
1 tablespoon (15 g) butter
1 onion, chopped
1 pound (500 g) pork (half fat, half lean), ground
½ pound (250 g) veal, ground
½ pound (250 g) chicken livers, finely chopped
2 cloves garlic, finely chopped
¼ teaspoon ground allspice
Pinch of ground ginger
Pinch of ground cloves
2 small eggs, beaten to mix
2 tablespoons brandy
Salt and freshly ground black pepper
½ cup (75 g) shelled pistachios—optional
1 slice cooked ham (about ½ pound or 250 g), cut in strips
1 bay leaf
1 sprig thyme

For the Luting Paste:
⅓ cup (50 g) flour
2–3 tablespoons water

*Terrine or casserole (2 quart or 2 L capacity)
with tight-fitting lid*

The recipe serves 8.

Line the terrine or casserole with barding fat or bacon, reserving a few slices for the top. Preheat oven to 350°F (175°C). Melt the butter in a small pan and sauté the onion until soft but not brown. Mix it with the pork, veal, livers, garlic, allspice, ginger, cloves, eggs, brandy and plenty of salt and pepper. Blend thoroughly. Sauté a small piece and taste for seasoning—the mixture should be quite spicy. Add the pistachios and beat until the mixture holds together. Spread a third of it in the lined terrine, add a layer of half the ham strips and top with another third of the pork mixture. Add the rest of the ham and cover with the remaining ground meat. Arrange the reserved bacon slices on top, trimming if necessary. Set the bay leaf and thyme on the bacon and cover.

For the luting paste: In a cup or bowl, lightly stir the water into the flour to make a paste; do not beat the paste or it will become elastic. Seal the gap between mold and lid with the paste.

Set the terrine in a water bath, bring to a boil on top of the stove and cook in the heated oven 1¼–1½ hours or until a skewer inserted for 30 seconds into the mixture through the hole in the terrine is hot to the touch when withdrawn. NOTE: regulate the heat so the water keeps simmering, adding more if necessary. Cool until tepid, remove the luting paste and lid and press the pâté with a board or plate and a 2 pound (1 kg) weight until cold. The pâté can be refrigerated up to a week or up to 3 months in the freezer. It may be served directly from the mold or on a platter.

Shrimp Pâté
PATE DE CREVETTES

A simple standby in which the full flavor of the shrimp comes through. Try it also with fresh crabmeat.

> 1 pound (500 g) cooked, peeled shrimps
> Juice of ½ lemon
> ½ cup (125 g) butter
> 2 tablespoons sherry or Madeira
> Salt and freshly ground black pepper
> Pinch of grated nutmeg
> Hot toast (for serving)

Work the shrimps with the lemon juice a little at a time in an electric food processor or blender; they should be coarsely chopped, not puréed. Cream the butter, stir in the shrimps and season to taste with sherry or Madeira, salt, pepper and nutmeg.

Pile the pâté in individual ramekins or a serving crock, cover tightly and chill. If to be kept more than 3–4 hours, smooth the top and add a thin layer of clarified butter to seal the pâté before chilling. Serve with hot toast.

Fish Fricassée with Limes and Ginger

FRICASSEE DE POISSON AU CITRON VERT ET AU GINGEMBRE

Nouvelle cuisine includes many new combinations, and this is one of the best—lightly poached fish with a stimulating sauce of lime and fresh ginger.

2 pound (1 kg) piece of monkfish, with the bones
Fish stock (see **Stuffed Sole with Whiskey Sauce**)
Salt and pepper
Pinch of thyme
Juice of 1 lemon
1 tablespoon oil
2 lemons
3 limes
1 tablespoon (15 g) butter
4 spring onions, thinly sliced
½ cup (1.25 dl) white wine

To Finish the Sauce:
2 tablespoons heavy cream
1 cup (250 g) butter
½ teaspoon grated fresh ginger or pinch of powdered ginger
Salt and pepper
2 tablespoons chopped parsley

The fricassée can also be prepared with eel, conger eel, sea bass, turbot or any firm, white fish.

Fillet the fish and use the bones for the fish stock. Cut the fish into 2″ (5 cm) chunks and wash thoroughly. Dry well, sprinkle with salt, pepper, thyme, lemon juice and oil and leave to marinate about 1 hour.

Pare the rind of the lemons, being careful not to include the bitter pith. Chop the rind into the tiniest pieces possible and blanch it: put in a saucepan of cold water, bring to a boil and boil 3–4 minutes or until tender. Refresh under cold running water, drain thoroughly and reserve. Peel the rind and all the pith of the limes, cut the flesh into thin slices and reserve.

In a sauté pan or shallow saucepan melt 1 tablespoon (15 g) butter, add the onions and cook slowly 5–7 minutes or until soft but not brown. Add the fish and cook gently with the onions, stirring, 2–3 minutes. Add the white wine and enough fish stock to cover, bring to a boil and simmer about 10 minutes or until just tender. Remove the pieces of fish and reserve. The fish can be cooked up to 24 hours ahead and kept covered in the refrigerator, but it should be slightly undercooked to allow for reheating.

To finish: Reheat the fish if necessary in a little fish stock, taking care not to overcook it. Keep warm in a serving bowl. Boil the fish cooking liquid and any remaining fish stock about 10 minutes or until reduced to 2–3 tablespoons. Add the cream and reduce again. Beat in the butter gradually in small pieces. Work sometimes over very low heat and sometimes off the heat, so that the butter softens and thickens the sauce without melting. Stir in the blanched lemon rind, lime slices and ginger with salt and pepper to taste. Add the chopped parsley and spoon the sauce over the fish. Serve immediately.

Shrimp Newburg
CREVETTES NEWBURG

The style of Shrimp Newburg, with its rich cream sauce, is typically French, though its origin is American. Shrimp Newburg is cooked the same way as Lobster Newburg, which started life in the 1890s at Delmonico's as Lobster Wenburg. The name was changed to Newburg when Mr. Wenburg and Mr. Delmonico had a disagreement.

½ cup (125 g) butter
1½ pounds (750 g) cooked, peeled large shrimps or scampi
½ teaspoon paprika
Salt and pepper
⅓ cup (1 dl) brandy or ½ cup (1.25 dl) Madeira
2 cups (5 dl) heavy cream
6 egg yolks

For the Rice Pilaf:
3 tablespoons (45 g) butter
1 onion, finely chopped
1½ cups (300 g) long-grained rice
3 cups (7.5 dl) water
Salt and pepper

1 quart (1 L) ring mold

This is one of the few hot recipes that calls for cooked shellfish; if the shrimp are raw, they should be simmered 4–5 minutes in salted water, then drained and peeled.

For the rice pilaf: In a heavy-based pan melt 2 tablespoons (30 g) butter and cook the onion until soft but not brown. Add the rice and sauté about 2 minutes, stirring, until the grains look transparent. Add the water, salt and pepper. Top with a round of buttered parchment paper, cover and bring to a boil. Simmer on top of the stove or in a 350°F (175°C) oven for exactly 18 minutes. If the liquid has evaporated but the rice is not cooked, add more water and cook a few more minutes until tender. Let the pilaf cool 10 minutes. Stir with a fork, add the 1 tablespoon (15 g) remaining butter and taste for seasoning. Butter the mold and fill it with rice, pressing it down lightly. Keep warm.

In a sauté pan or chafing dish, melt 3 tablespoons (45 g) butter. Add the shrimps, sprinkle with paprika, season, cover and heat gently 2–3 minutes. Add the brandy or Madeira and flame. Take from the heat and keep warm. Stir the cream into the egg yolks, add to the pan and heat gently, shaking the pan until the sauce thickens. NOTE: do not allow it to get too hot, or it will curdle. Off the heat add the remaining butter in small pieces, shaking the pan until the butter is softened and mixed in. Taste for seasoning.

Turn out the rice ring onto a platter and spoon the shrimps into the center, serving any remaining sauce separately.

Chicken and Shrimp Sauté à L'Indienne
SAUTE DE POULET ET CREVETTES A L'INDIENNE

Indienne in French cooking always refers to a seasoning of curry powder. Here the piquancy can be increased by adding more cayenne.

2 tablespoons (30 g) butter
1½ tablespoons oil
Salt and freshly ground black pepper
2½–3 pound (1–1.5 kg) broiling chicken, cut in 5 or 6 pieces
1 onion, thinly sliced
1 clove garlic, crushed
1 teaspoon curry powder, or to taste
Pinch of cayenne
1 cup (2.5 dl) chicken stock
Pinch of saffron, soaked in ¼ cup (6 cl) boiling stock
   for 15 minutes
½ pound (250 g) cooked, peeled shrimps
1½ cups (300 g) rice (for serving)
Chutney and grated fresh coconut—optional

The recipe serves 3–4.

In a sauté pan or skillet heat the butter and oil. Season the pieces of chicken and add to the pan, cut side down, starting with the legs and thighs because they need the longest cooking. When they begin to brown, add the wing and breast pieces. When all are brown, turn them over and brown the other side for 2 minutes. Remove from the pan. Add the onion and cook slowly until soft but not brown. Add the garlic, curry powder and cayenne pepper and cook gently, stirring, 2 minutes. Return the chicken pieces to the pan. Add the stock and saffron, cover and simmer 15–20 minutes until the chicken is nearly tender. Stir in the shrimps and simmer 5 more minutes. The sauté can be prepared up to 3 days ahead and kept covered in the refrigerator, or it can be frozen.

To finish: Reheat the sauté on top of the stove, if necessary. Boil 3 quarts (3 L) salted water, add the rice and boil, stirring occasionally with a fork, 10–12 minutes or until the rice is tender but still resistant to the teeth. Drain and rinse thoroughly with hot water. Spoon the rice down one side of a platter, arrange the pieces of chicken down the other and garnish with the shrimps. Reduce the sauce, if necessary, to 5–6 tablespoons and taste for seasoning—it should be piquant but not overpowering. Spoon it over the chicken and serve. Chutney and grated coconut are good accompaniments.

Chicken Fricassée with Mushrooms and Baby Onions

FRICASSEE DE POULET A L'ANCIENNE

This traditional fricassée, with its flour and egg-yolk enriched sauce and garnish of onions and mushrooms, is an interesting contrast to the new trends demonstrated by **Fish Fricassée with Limes and Ginger.**

3 tablespoons (45 g) butter
3½–4 pound (1.5–2 kg) roasting chicken, cut in 5 or 6 pieces
2 tablespoons (15 g) flour
2½–3 cups (6.25–7.5 dl) chicken stock
Salt and white pepper
Bouquet garni
1 tablespoon chopped parsley (for sprinkling)

For the Garnish:
16–18 baby onions, peeled
2 tablespoons (30 g) butter
½ cup (1.25 dl) chicken stock
Salt and pepper
½ pound (250 g) mushrooms, quartered

For the Liaison:
3 egg yolks
½ cup (1.25 dl) heavy cream

In a sauté pan or skillet melt the butter and add the pieces of chicken, skin side down. Cook over low heat until the meat is stiffened and white; this should take about 10 minutes. Remove the pieces, sprinkle in the flour and cook, stirring, 1–2 minutes until foaming but not brown. Add 2½ cups (6.25 dl) stock with salt, pepper and the bouquet garni and bring to a boil, stirring. Replace the pieces of chicken, cover and cook over low heat on top of the stove or in a 350°F (175°C) oven, stirring occasionally, 25–30 minutes or until tender. If the sauce gets too thick, add more stock.

For the garnish: Put the onions in a pan with 1 tablespoon (15 g) butter, ¼ cup (6 cl) stock, salt and pepper and cover tightly. Cook over low heat, shaking the pan occasionally, 12–15 minutes or until tender. Put the mushrooms in a pan with the remaining butter and stock, add salt and pepper, cover tightly and cook over very high heat until the liquid boils to the top of the pan. The chicken, onions and mushrooms can be cooked 24 hours ahead and kept covered, in separate containers, in the refrigerator.

To finish: Reheat the chicken if necessary, transfer to a platter and keep warm. Discard the bouquet garni, add the liquid from cooking the onions and mushrooms to the pan and reduce the sauce, if necessary, until it coats a spoon. Add the onions and mushrooms and heat thoroughly. *For the liaison:* Mix the yolks and cream in a bowl, stir in a little of the hot sauce and stir this mixture back into the remaining sauce. Heat gently, shaking the pan, until the sauce thickens slightly. NOTE: do not boil or it will curdle. Coat the chicken with the sauce, spoon the garnish around it and sprinkle with parsley. Serve the remaining sauce separately.

Duck Steak with Green Peppercorns
MAGRET DE CANARD AU POIVRE VERT

Magrets are boneless duck breasts. They are an unusual alternative to steak and lend themselves to similar, robust seasonings.

Breasts of 1 duck
1 tablespoon oil
1 tablespoon (15 g) butter
Salt and freshly ground black pepper

For the Sauce:
3 shallots, finely chopped
1½ cups (3.75 dl) red wine
2 teaspoons meat glaze
2 tablespoons heavy cream
1 teaspoon green peppercorns, drained and crushed
1 tablespoon (15 g) butter (to finish)

The recipe serves 2.

To remove the breasts from a duck: Using a sharp knife, remove the wishbone. Remove each breast by sliding the knife between the meat and the bone. Leave the skin on the two breasts or remove it, as you prefer. Cut off the wing bone.

In a heavy skillet, heat the oil and butter. Season the duck breasts with salt and pepper and fry over fairly high heat, allowing about 3 minutes on each side for rare meat. The meat should be well browned. The magrets can be served whole, halved or sliced. Transfer to a platter and keep warm.

For the sauce: Add the chopped shallots to the pan and cook gently 1 minute. Add the wine, stir to dissolve the pan juices and boil until reduced by half. Add the meat glaze, cream and green peppercorns and cook 2–3 minutes. Drain any juice from the duck into the sauce. Remove the sauce from the heat and swirl in the butter, a little at a time. Taste for seasoning. Pour the sauce over the duck pieces and serve.

Duck Ragoût with Madeira

RAGOUT DE CANARD AU MADERE

One of Anne's favorite demonstration menus makes full use of a duck. The legs are used in this ragoût, the breast makes steak with green peppercorns, and the skin and liver go into a hot salad (see **Duck Steak with Green Peppercorns** *and* **Duck Skin and Liver Salad***).*

1 large duck (4–5 pounds or 2–2.5 kg) or 4 duck legs
1 tablespoon oil
1 onion, chopped
1½ tablespoons (10 g) flour
¾ cup (2 dl) red wine
¾–1 cup (2–2.5 dl) stock
Bouquet garni
2 shallots, chopped
1 clove garlic, crushed
Salt and freshly ground black pepper
¼ pound (125 g) mushrooms, thinly sliced
3 tablespoons Madeira
1 tablespoon chopped parsley (for garnish)

For the Croûtes:
3 slices bread, crusts removed, cut in triangles
4 tablespoons (60 g) oil and butter, mixed (for frying)

Cut the duck in quarters, discarding the backbone. In a sauté pan or skillet heat the oil and sauté the pieces of duck or the duck legs, cut side down, 15–20 minutes or until well browned and rendered of all fat. NOTE: this must be done thoroughly or the finished dish will be greasy. Remove the duck and pour off all but 2 tablespoons fat. Add the onion and cook until lightly browned. Stir in the flour and cook, stirring, until browned. Pour in the wine and stock and add the bouquet garni, shallots, garlic, salt and pepper. Replace the duck, cover and simmer 15–20 minutes or until tender, adding more stock if the sauce gets thick.

Take out the duck and trim the leg and knuckle bones with scissors. Strain the sauce into a pan, skim off any fat, add the mushrooms and Madeira and simmer 2–3 minutes. Replace the duck and taste the sauce for seasoning. The duck can be cooked 48 hours ahead; keep it in its sauce in the refrigerator. It can also be frozen.

To finish: Reheat the duck on top of the stove. *For the croûtes:* Brown the bread on both sides in the oil and butter and drain on paper towels. Arrange the duck on a platter, spoon over the mushrooms and sauce and place the croûtes on the edge of the dish. Sprinkle the duck with parsley and serve.

Beef Fillet Cherniavsky
FILET DE BOEUF CHERNIAVSKY

Cherniavsky is Anne's married name. She developed this dish, which can be prepared ahead, for dinner parties.

3–4 pound (1.5–2 kg) beef fillet, trimmed and tied with string
Salt and freshly ground black pepper
1 tablespoon oil
2 tablespoons chopped parsley (for sprinkling)

For the Stuffing:
2 shallots
4 ounces (125 g) bacon
1 pound (500 g) mushrooms, finely chopped
4 large tomatoes (2 pounds or 1 kg), peeled, seeded
    and chopped
Salt and freshly ground black pepper

For the Madeira Sauce:
3 cups (7.5 dl) brown veal stock
2 tablespoons (20 g) arrowroot or potato starch
½ cup (1.25 dl) Madeira
Salt and freshly ground black pepper

The recipe serves 8–10.

Set the oven at 450°F (230°C). Sprinkle the beef with salt and pepper. Heat the oil until very hot and brown the meat well on all sides. Roast the meat in the very hot oven for 11 minutes. Remove to a dish and leave to cool. Discard the fat from the pan.

For the stuffing: In an electric food processor chop the shallots and bacon together to a fine paste. In a skillet or sauté pan heat the shallot and bacon paste 1–2 minutes. Add the chopped mushrooms, mix well and add the tomatoes, salt and pepper. Cook over high heat, stirring often, 15–18 minutes or until all moisture has evaporated. Taste for seasoning and leave to cool completely.

When the beef fillet is cool, remove the strings. Slice it in ¾" (2 cm) slices, leaving each slice attached at the bottom. Spread 1–2 tablespoons stuffing on each slice and press the fillet back into its original shape. Wrap the beef in two layers of aluminum foil and tie with string. The beef can be prepared ahead up to this point and kept 1–2 days in the refrigerator. Keep any remaining stuffing in a bowl and store, covered, in the refrigerator.

For the sauce: Bring the brown stock to a boil. Mix the arrowroot or potato starch to a paste with half the Madeira. Pour the mixture into the stock, whisking constantly, adding enough to thicken the sauce so it lightly coats a spoon. Add the remaining Madeira, or to taste, strain if necessary, bring just back to a boil and taste for seasoning.

To finish: Allow the beef to come to room temperature. Set the oven at 425°F (220°C). Put the beef, still wrapped in the foil, in a roasting pan and reheat in the oven 15 minutes or until the filling is hot. Leave the wrapped fillet in a warm place until ready to serve. Reheat the extra stuffing and spread a layer down the center of an oval platter.

To serve: Unwrap the beef, saving the juices that escape, and set it on the stuffing on the platter. Add the juices to the sauce, bring to a boil and spoon it over the beef. Sprinkle with chopped parsley.

Veal Escalopes with Roquefort

ESCALOPES DE VEAU AU ROQUEFORT

Roquefort in a cooked dish gives an unexpected tang, but be sure not to overseason since the cheese is quite salty itself.

> 1½ pounds (750 g) veal escalopes
> ½ cup (75 g) flour
> 3 tablespoons (45 g) butter, or half oil and half butter
> 1 cup (2.5 dl) heavy cream
> 1 teaspoon meat glaze—optional
> ½ cup (100 g) Roquefort cheese, crumbled
> Salt—optional—and pepper

Put each escalope between two sheets of waxed paper and pound it with a meat mallet or cleaver to flatten. Coat them with flour, patting to remove the excess.

In a sauté pan or skillet heat the butter or mixture of oil and butter and fry the escalopes over medium heat until browned, allowing 2–3 minutes on each side. Arrange them overlapping on a platter and keep warm. Deglaze the pan with the cream and simmer until slightly reduced. Add the meat glaze and the cheese, whisking constantly over low heat until smooth. Add salt if necessary and pepper and strain. Pour over the escalopes and serve.

Shoulder of Lamb à la Turque
EPAULE D'AGNEAU A LA TURQUE

Anne has made this dish in half a dozen different places, and in each, she says, the meat was quite different. In Australia the mammoth whole shoulder took 40 minutes to bone, in Italy the lamb was so tiny she could operate only with a little vegetable knife, and in Texas it proved impossible to find a shoulder with any bones left in at all! But when tied and strung, each of the differing meats produced a relatively inexpensive, yet impressive roast.

4–5 pound (2–2.5 kg) shoulder of lamb, boned (bones reserved)
1 tablespoon oil
1 onion, quartered
1 carrot, quartered
1–2 cloves garlic, peeled and cut in slivers
1 teaspoon rosemary
Salt and freshly ground black pepper
½ cup (1.25 dl) white wine
1 cup (2.5 dl) brown stock

For the Stuffing:
2 tablespoons (30 g) butter
1 medium onion, finely chopped
1 cup (200 g) rice
2 cups (5 dl) water
½ cup (50 g) raisins
Salt and freshly ground black pepper
½ cup (75 g) pine nuts, or ¾ cup (100 g) whole
   blanched almonds
2 tablespoons chopped parsley
2 eggs

Trussing needle and string

Shoulder of Lamb à la Turque is good served with **Stuffed Eggplant Imam Bayeldi** and **Provençal Tomatoes.** Any leftover rice stuffing can be reheated to serve separately.

For the stuffing: In a casserole melt the butter and cook the onion slowly until soft but not brown. Add the rice and cook, stirring, until the grains are transparent. Add the water with the raisins, salt and pepper, cover and bring to a boil. Simmer on top of the stove or in a 350 °F (175 °C) oven for exactly 18 minutes. Leave 10 minutes to cool before removing the lid. Stir to separate the grains and cool to tepid. If using almonds, bake them in a 400°F (200°C) oven for 4–6 minutes until golden brown. Stir the pine nuts or almonds, parsley and eggs into the rice and taste—it should be highly seasoned. Fill the pocket in the lamb with stuffing and sew up with string to a cushion shape. The lamb can be stuffed up to 6 hours before cooking if the stuffing is cold before it is put inside the meat.

One and a half to two hours before serving: Set the oven at 400°F (200°C). Put the oil in the roasting pan, add the lamb bones, onion and carrot and put the lamb on top. Make several incisions in the meat with the point of a knife and insert the garlic slivers. Sprinkle the meat with rosemary, salt and pepper and roast, basting often, for 1¼–1½ hours. Transfer the lamb to a platter and let rest in a warm place 15 minutes before carving. Discard the excess fat from the pan but leave in the bones, onion and carrot. Deglaze the pan juices with the wine, reduce by half and add the stock. Simmer briefly, strain into a small saucepan, bring back to a boil and taste for seasoning. Serve separately.

Provençal Tomatoes
TOMATES PROVENÇALE

Colorful, quick to make, these tomatoes with a touch of garlic are an invaluable garnish for any meat or poultry dish.

>   4 large tomatoes
>   3 tablespoons browned breadcrumbs
>   1 clove garlic, chopped
>   1 tablespoon chopped parsley
>   Salt and freshly ground black pepper
>   2 tablespoons (30 g) butter or olive oil

Cut the tomatoes in half and cut out the cores. Put them in a buttered baking dish. Combine the breadcrumbs, garlic, parsley, salt and pepper and add the melted butter or oil to form a crumbly mixture. Spoon the mixture into the tomatoes. The tomatoes can be prepared up to 12 hours ahead and kept in the refrigerator.

To finish: Bake the tomatoes in a 375°F (190°C) oven 12–15 minutes until just tender.

Eggplant Terrine
TERRINE D'AUBERGINES

Vegetable terrines are very much in vogue. This dish, combining eggplant, zucchini, green peppers and tomatoes with a good measure of olive oil and garlic is like a molded ratatouille.

4 small eggplants (total weight 2 pounds or 1 kg)
6 tablespoons (1 dl) olive oil or vegetable oil
4 zucchini, sliced in thick rounds
3 onions, chopped
4 cloves garlic, finely chopped
2 red peppers, diced
3 green peppers, diced
3 tomatoes, peeled, seeded and chopped
Bouquet garni
Salt and freshly ground black pepper
1 egg
⅓–½ cup (40–50 g) breadcrumbs

For the Tomato Coulis:
1 pound (500 g) tomatoes, peeled, seeded and chopped
Salt and pepper

Terrine with lid (2 quart or 2 L capacity)

The recipe serves 6–8.

Set the oven at 425°F (220°C). Halve the eggplants lengthwise, score the cut side with a knife and bake in an oiled pan 15–20 minutes or until the flesh is somewhat softened. Remove the pulp with a spoon, being careful not to pierce the skin. Set the oven at 350°F (175°C). In a skillet heat 2 tablespoons oil and sauté the zucchini rounds until slightly browned.

For the tomato coulis: In a heavy-based saucepan over low heat cook the tomatoes with salt and pepper, covered, for 10 minutes. Uncover and simmer, stirring occasionally, about 15 minutes or until very thick.

In a large heavy-based pan heat the remaining oil, add the onions and cook slowly until soft but not brown. Add the garlic, peppers, sautéed zucchini, eggplant pulp, tomato coulis, tomatoes, bouquet garni, salt and pepper and cook uncovered 25-30 minutes or until all the vegetables are tender and the mixture is thick. Discard the bouquet garni. Take from the heat and add the egg and enough breadcrumbs to make a mixture stiff enough to hold together though not dry. Taste for seasoning.

Butter the terrine generously and line it with the eggplant skins, purple sides outwards. Spoon in the mixture. Cover the terrine and put in a water bath. Bring to a boil on top of the stove and bake in the oven for one hour or until firm. Cool about 15 minutes and unmold. Serve hot or cold.

Potatoes Darphin
POMMES DARPHIN

Anne likes to use this potato cake as a base for poultry dishes such as **Chicken Fricassée with Mushrooms and Baby Onions** *and* **Duck Ragoût with Madeira**.

> 2 pounds (1 kg) baking potatoes, peeled
> 2 tablespoons oil
> ¼ cup (60 g) butter
> Salt and freshly ground black pepper
>
> *7–8" (18–20 cm) heavy frying pan*

Cut the peeled potatoes into julienne strips and dry thoroughly on paper towels. NOTE: do not soak in water as this removes some of the starch, which is necessary in this dish to stick the potatoes together. Spread the oil and half the butter over the base and sides of the pan and press in a thick layer of potatoes. Dot with butter and lightly sprinkle with salt and pepper. Add the remaining potatoes, lightly seasoning each layer, and mound them well. Cover the pan with buttered foil, tucking down the sides to prevent steam escaping. Cover and put a weight on top. Set the oven at 375°F (190°C).

Cook the potatoes over low heat 10 minutes or until the bottom is browned. To check, lift up one side of the potatoes with a metal spatula— you should smell browned butter. Bake for 30 more minutes or until very tender. The potatoes can be cooked up to 12 hours ahead and kept in the pan at room temperature.

To finish: If necessary, reheat the potatoes on top of the stove. Loosen the base of the cake with a metal spatula and turn it out on a platter. Cut in wedges to serve.

Baked Zucchini
COURGETTES AU GRATIN

This is one of the few hot zucchini recipes that can be prepared ahead.

> 1 pound (500 g) zucchini, cut in ½" (1 cm) diagonal slices
> Salt and pepper
> 2 eggs
> 1 cup (2.5 dl) heavy cream
> ¼ cup (30 g) grated Gruyère cheese

Blanch the zucchini in boiling salted water for 5 minutes and drain well. Spread them in a buttered shallow baking dish. Beat the eggs with the cream and seasoning. Pour this custard over the zucchini and sprinkle with cheese. The zucchini can be prepared up to 6 hours ahead.

To finish: Bake in a 400°F (200°C) oven for 10–15 minutes until the custard is just set and the top is browned.

Duck Skin and Liver Salad
SALADE DE PEAU ET FOIE DE CANARD

Robust greens like escarole are best for this unusual salad with a hot dressing.

Skin from breast of 1 fat duck
4 duck or chicken livers, halved
1 head escarole, curly chicory, or 1½ pounds (750 g)
   dandelion leaves
Salt and freshly ground black pepper
1 clove garlic, very finely chopped
2 tablespoons wine vinegar

For the Croûtons:
3–4 slices white bread, crusts removed, diced, OR
   ½ loaf French bread, thinly sliced and cut in
   triangular pieces
6 tablespoons (1 dl) oil (if using white bread)
1 clove garlic (if using French bread)

For the croutons: If using white bread, fry the diced bread in oil until golden brown and pour into a strainer to drain. The croûtons can be made 2–3 hours ahead and kept at room temperature. If using French bread, rub the pieces with a cut clove of garlic; do not fry.

Using a sharp knife, remove the skin from the duck breast and cut into small pieces. Trim any green spots from the livers. Wash the greens, trim the stalks of dandelion leaves and dry thoroughly. Place in a salad bowl and season with salt, pepper and chopped garlic.

In a frying pan, fry the duck skin until well browned and crisp. With a slotted spoon transfer the skin to the salad. Discard all but 4 tablespoons fat from the pan and reheat until very hot. Season the livers, add to the hot fat and sauté over very high heat ½–1 minute on each side, or until well browned on the outside but still pink inside. Pour them with the hot fat over the salad. Add the vinegar to the pan, bring to a boil, pour over the leaves and toss until they wilt slightly. Add the croûtons, taste for seasoning and serve at once while still lukewarm.

Peaches or Strawberries Cardinal
PECHES OU FRAISES CARDINAL

This dessert is simplicity itself, and when fresh peaches or strawberries are in season, it can't be beaten. Cardinal refers to the brilliant red of the raspberry sauce.

6–8 ripe freestone peaches, or 1½ quarts (750 g) strawberries

For Poaching Peaches:
⅔ cup (125 g) sugar
2 cups (5 dl) water
Pared rind and juice of 1 lemon
Vanilla bean

For the Raspberry Sauce:
1 quart (500 g) fresh raspberries, or 1 pound (500 g)
    frozen raspberries, thawed
1 tablespoon kirsch
3–4 tablespoons confectioners' sugar, or to taste

The recipe serves 6.

If using peaches, make a syrup by heating the sugar in the water until dissolved and adding the lemon rind and juice and vanilla bean. Halve the peaches, discarding the pits, and immerse in the syrup, cut side up. NOTE: if the peaches are large, they may need cooking in two batches. Poach 8–12 minutes or until just tender, leave to cool in the syrup and then drain, reserving the syrup. Peel the peaches. If using strawberries, hull them and wash if sandy.

For the sauce: Purée the raspberries in a blender with the kirsch and confectioners' sugar, adding a little of the reserved syrup from cooking the peaches to fresh raspberries to make a sauce of coating consistency. NOTE: the sauce should be quite sweet to balance the tartness of the fruit. Strain it to remove the seeds.

Pile the peaches or strawberries in a glass bowl, pour over the sauce so the fruit is completely coated, cover tightly and chill at least 2 hours and up to 8 hours so the fruit absorbs the flavor of the sauce.

Strawberry Charlotte Malakoff

CHARLOTTE MALAKOFF AUX FRAISES

A malakoff mixture is always based on ground almonds. It can be flavored with kirsch, with coffee, with candied fruits and cointreau, or with straw-berries as here.

12–14 ladyfingers (see **Ladyfingers**)
2 tablespoons kirsch
1 cup (125 g) whole blanched almonds
½ cup (125 g) unsalted butter
⅔ cup (125 g) sugar
1 pint (200 g) fresh strawberries, hulled and cut in pieces
½ cup (1.25 dl) heavy cream, whipped until it holds
    a soft shape
Raspberry sauce—optional (see **Peaches or**
    Strawberries Cardinal)

For Decoration:
½ cup (1.25 dl) heavy cream
2 teaspoons sugar
½ teaspoon vanilla extract
A few whole strawberries—optional

Charlotte mold or soufflé dish (5 cups or
    1.25 L capacity)
Pastry bag with medium star tube

Butter the mold or dish, line its base with a circle of waxed paper and butter it also. Line the sides with ladyfingers, trimming them to fit tightly. Sprinkle the remaining ladyfingers with 2 tablespoons kirsch. Grind the almonds a few at a time in a blender or with a rotary cheese grater.

Cream the butter, gradually beat in the sugar and continue beating un-til very soft and light. Stir in the ground almonds, remaining kirsch and strawberries. Do not beat or the oil will be drawn out of the almonds. Fold in the lightly whipped cream and spoon half the mixture into the mold. Cover with soaked ladyfingers, add remaining almond mixture and smooth the top. Cover and chill the charlotte at least 4 hours or until firm-ly set. It can be made 3–4 days ahead and kept in the refrigerator.

To finish: Not more than 2 hours before serving, trim the edges of the ladyfingers level with the almond mixture. Unmold the charlotte onto a platter. In a chilled bowl, whip the cream until it starts to thicken. Add the sugar and vanilla and continue beating until the cream holds a shape. Using a pastry bag and a medium star tube, cover the top and base with rosettes of whipped cream. Add whole strawberries. Serve with raspberry sauce.

Chocolate Snowball
BOULE DE NEIGE

"Don't count calories when picking dessert," says Anne, and it is hard to imagine anything richer than this mold made with almost equal weights of chocolate, butter, sugar and eggs. A generous coating of whipped cream is the final touch, or should we say the final blow.

8 ounces (250 g) sweet chocolate, chopped
½ cup (1.25 dl) strong, black coffee, or 2 teaspoons
    instant coffee dissolved in ½ cup (1.25 dl) warm water
1 cup (250 g) unsalted butter
1 cup (200 g) sugar
4 eggs, beaten to mix

For Decoration:
1½ cups (3.75 dl) heavy cream
1–2 tablespoons sugar
2–3 teaspoons brandy
Candied violets

Charolotte mold or deep metal mold (4–5 cup or
   1–1.25 L capacity)
Pastry bag with medium star tube

The recipe serves 6–8.

Line the mold with a double thickness of foil. Set the oven at 350°F (175°C). In a heavy-based pan melt the chocolate in the coffee over low heat. Add the butter and sugar a little at a time, stirring after each addition until melted. Heat until very hot but do not boil. Take from the heat and beat in the eggs a little at a time. Strain into the prepared mold and bake 30–40 minutes or until a thick crust has formed on top. The mixture will rise slightly, but will fall again as it cools. Let cool, then cover and keep at least 3 days or up to 2 weeks in the refrigerator.

Not more than 3 hours before serving, run a knife around the mold and turn it out onto a platter. Peel off the foil—the mixture tends to stick and will look messy at this point.

For decoration: In a chilled bowl whip the cream until it starts to thicken. Add the sugar and brandy and continue beating until the cream holds a shape. Be careful not to overbeat. Using a pastry bag fitted with a medium star tube, cover the mold completely with whipped cream rosettes so no chocolate shows. Crown it with a single, larger rosette and stud the top and sides with candied violets. Chill until serving.

Hot Lemon Soufflé

SOUFFLE CHAUD AU CITRON

Anne is a lover of soufflés. Like her recipe for cheese soufflé, this lemon mixture is extra light as it contains no flour.

> ¼ cup (60 g) unsalted butter
> ⅔ cup (125 g) sugar
> ⅓ cup (1 dl) lemon juice
> 4 egg yolks
> Grated rind of 2 lemons
> 5 egg whites
> Confectioners' sugar (for sprinkling)
>
> *Soufflé dish (1 quart or 1 L capacity)*

Butter the soufflé dish and sprinkle with sugar, discarding the excess. In a heavy-based pan (not aluminum) heat the butter with ¼ cup (50 g) sugar and the lemon juice until the butter and sugar melt. Take from the heat and beat in the yolks, one by one. Add the lemon rind. Heat very gently, stirring constantly, until the mixture thickens to the consistency of heavy cream. NOTE: do not let it get too hot or it will curdle. The soufflé can be prepared 3–4 hours ahead to this point. Keep covered at room temperature.

Twenty to thirty minutes before serving: Set the oven at 425°F (220°C). Whip the whites until stiff, preferably in a copper bowl. Add the remaining sugar and beat 20 seconds longer or until glossy. Gently heat the lemon mixture until hot to the touch and stir in about a quarter of the egg whites. Add this mixture to the remaining whites and fold together as lightly as possible. Spoon into the prepared dish and bake at once in preheated oven for 12–15 minutes or until puffed and brown. Sprinkle with confectioners' sugar and serve at once.

Iced Coffee Soufflé

SOUFFLE GLACE AU CAFE

This recipe is guaranteed to give a superbly smooth iced dessert without using an ice cream churn. Coffee is just one of several possible flavorings. The soufflé mixture is often layered with crushed meringue.

⅔ cup (125 g) sugar
⅓ cup (1 dl) water
2 egg whites
¾ cup (2 dl) heavy cream, whipped until it holds a soft peak
1–1½ tablespoons instant coffee dissolved in 3 tablespoons warm water

For Decoration:
½ cup (1.25 dl) heavy cream, whipped until stiff
4 browned almonds, pecan or walnut halves, or candied violets

4 parfait glasses, or heavy-stemmed glasses, or 4 small ramekins
Pastry bag with medium star tube

If using ramekins, wrap a collar of foil or waxed paper around each to extend 1½–2" (4–5 cm) above the edge of the dish and tie with string. Place in the freezer until ready to use.

Heat the sugar with the water over low heat until dissolved. Bring to a boil and boil without stirring until the syrup reaches the soft ball stage (239°F or 115°C on a sugar thermometer). NOTE: while the syrup boils, wash down any sugar crystals from the sides of the pan with a brush dipped in water. Meanwhile, beat the egg whites until stiff. Gradually pour the hot sugar syrup over them, beating constantly, and continue beating at high speed until the meringue is cold and very stiff.

Carefully fold in the lightly whipped cream with dissolved coffee to taste. Spoon the mixture into glasses or prepared ramekins, smoothing the top. Freeze at least 4 hours or until firm. It can be kept in the freezer, tightly covered, for 2–3 months.

To finish: Using a pastry bag and medium star tube, top each soufflé with a rosette of whipped cream and a nut or candied violet. Discard the collars from the ramekins. If the soufflés have been frozen for more than 24 hours, let them soften 1–2 hours in the refrigerator before serving.

Trifle

TRIFLE

Anne was brought up in Yorkshire, a rural part of England where this dessert is a perennial favorite. It is not a trifling dish at all, but a robust mixture of cake, poached fruit, egg custard and whipped cream.

1 pound (500 g) sponge cake or pound cake
½ jar (6 ounces or 180 g) raspberry jam
½ cup (1.25 dl) sherry
1 can (1 pound or 500 g) sliced pears or peaches, drained
1 cup (2.5 dl) heavy cream, whipped until stiff
¼ cup (50 g) whole blanched almonds, toasted

For the Custard:
3 cups (7.5 dl) milk
Vanilla bean, split, or 1 teaspoon vanilla extract
4 eggs
5 egg yolks
¾ cup (180 g) sugar

Glass bowl (1½ quart or 1.5 L capacity)
Pastry bag with medium star tube

The recipe serves 6–8.

Cut the cake in three layers, sandwich with raspberry jam and cut in 1" (2.5 cm) squares. Put squares in the bottom of the bowl, spoon in sherry and press down lightly. Add the drained fruit.

For the custard: Scald the milk with the vanilla bean (not the extract) and leave in a warm place to infuse 10–15 minutes. Beat the eggs and yolks with the sugar until light and fairly thick. Stir in half the hot milk and stir this mixture back into the remaining milk. Heat gently, stirring constantly, until the custard thickens slightly; when you draw your finger across the back of the spoon, it will leave a clear trail. Do not overcook or boil or the custard will curdle. Take at once from the heat and strain into a bowl. If using vanilla extract, add it now. Let cool to tepid. Pour the custard over the cake and fruit to completely cover. Cover and chill.

Not more than 3 hours before serving, cover the custard completely with small rosettes of whipped cream, using a pastry bag fitted with a star tube. Alternatively, make a lattice of cream so the custard shows through and pipe rosettes around the edge of the bowl. Top the rosettes with browned almonds.

INDEX
compiled by Janet Jones